Ian,
We hope this will
entice "Team Roberts" to
join us down under
sooner than later!
Happy Holidays to all
of you.
Lots of love,
Chris, Ali & Ben
Xmas 2011.

DESTINATION
TROUT
NEW ZEALAND

Kent Fraser and Adam Clancey

David Bateman

Published 2006 by David Bateman Ltd,
30 Tarndale Grove, Albany, Auckland,
New Zealand

Distributed in the United States by Stackpole
Books, 5067 Ritter Road, Mechanicsburg,
PA 17055

ISBN-13: 978-1-86953-617-6
ISBN-10: 1-86953-617-7

Cover design: Intesa Goup
Design and layout: Intesa Group
Printed in China through Colorcraft Ltd,
Hong Kong

CONTENTS

North Island

South Island

> 'Well, it is a plea to those of you who are adventurous to keep fighting, not to be discouraged when you are frustrated by the unadventurous, and to remember that adventure in any form can act as a most appetising spice for the flavourless gruel of modern civilised existence. Search for worthy objectives for your adventures then prosecute them with wisdom and judgement.'
>
> Dr Phillip Law

FOREWORD

It is my pleasure to write the foreword to *Destination Trout New Zealand*, a trout-fishing and travel guide with a difference. I hope you the reader will enjoy it as much as I have, and as much as Kent, Adam and the many other people who contributed to the project enjoyed the process of bringing it to you.

I first met Adam Clancey on a Northland rock ledge in the early eighties. But it wasn't until I moved to Auckland a few years later that we became more than acquaintances.

Adam was a young, enthusiastic angler who, not surprisingly, knocked around with other keen, enthusiastic young anglers. We shared mutual friends and our paths regularly crossed.

Later, Adam and I worked together producing a popular fishing magazine, before we each went our separate ways. During that time we became more than colleagues and remain friends.

Like most of us, Adam is not so young anymore, though – if it's possible – he is keener on fishing today than ever before. Better still, the last few years have allowed him to truly pursue his interests, sharing his enthusiasm with the rest of us through magazine articles, television programmes, DVDs and books.

Adam's friend and colleague, Kent Fraser, has managed to pack a lifetime's worth of adventuring and exotic fishing into the last 20 years, despite a busy international career in finance that has taken him all over the planet.

I met Kent through mutual fishing buddies when he was better known as 'Monkey'. Together, we enjoyed fishing expeditions around the Hauraki Gulf and beyond. Years later I was able to publish Kent's first article in *New Zealand Fisherman* magazine, one of many, it would turn out.

It was an enthusiastic and gripping account of an epic fishing expedition to a remote corner of Outer Mongolia, where he tackled huge fish in wild rivers and extreme weather. Later he wrote about mountain-biking and fishing expeditions to Mongolia and Sri Lanka, launched from his base in Shanghai, fishing and climbing in the Himalayas and more. Kent remains a man of action, a passionate traveller and photographer always searching for new challenges and keen to share his adventures and antics on the road less travelled, of which this book is one.

Kent and Adam have also joined forces as business partners and creative collaborators on several projects. Together they produce the popular Fishing NZ television programme, which screens on Sky TV.

Destination Trout New Zealand and the accompanying DVD is a logical progression for

ABOVE:
Malcolm Bell lands a beautiful brown for the camera.

OPPOSITE:
John Eichelsheim – ardent angler, prolific writer and keen traveller doing what he does best.

New Zealand is a fly fisher's paradise with rivers and lakes open to all visitors.

the pair. A compendium of great photos, world class fishing and breathtaking New Zealand landscapes with a wealth of first hand information on locations, attractions and activities, it is a refreshingly original take on a well travelled path – the New Zealand trout fishing guide.

This comprehensive book comprises only half the resource; each destination has been painstakingly captured in a truly expansive DVD production with amazing footage artfully mixed to an evocative original soundtrack from talented Kiwi musicians. This truly unique and original dual media production ushers in an exciting new standard in travel guides that provides tourists, travellers, and the keenest of thrill seekers and fly-fishing fanatics with essential information and hours of spectacular and uniquely Kiwi entertainment.

Every location featured in *Destination Trout* has been visited, fished, filmed and photographed, often in the company of local experts or fishing friends. The result is a destination guide and trout fishing travel companion unlike any other.

Some of the featured waters are exceedingly well known; many are not; some are recognised for their exceptional fishing; others are representative of 'ordinary' New Zealand lakes and streams. The superb quality of some of the fishing and the easy access of many of the locations presented will doubtless surprise some readers, but there is remote challenging water and challenging fishing as well.

The selection of angling locations in *Destination Trout* is personal: they are Kent and Adam's favourite waters. But in keeping with the pair's philosophy, the angling presented in this book is accessible for ordinary fishers, Kiwis and visitors alike.

With this book tucked under your arm, you'll have no trouble finding good, and sometimes great, trout fishing all over this wonderful country. Get out there and give it a go.

John Eichelsheim,
Auckland, April 2006

ACKNOWLEDGEMENTS

This book and the accompanying DVD represent the compilation of many years of personal experience, observation, adventure and mishap, and good fortune. However, it would not have been possible without valuable contributions and encouragement from a number of individuals and organisations. In particular, a huge thanks to our long-suffering wives and families who have tolerated our numerous absences and postponed home-improvement projects. Friends, anglers, hunters, mountaineers, trampers, farmers, New Zealand Fish and Game, the Department of Conservation and Biosecurity New Zealand have all made special contributions and we would like to thank them all individually. Special thanks to Maui Campervans, Composite Developments, TUMONZ and The Complete Angler Store who have waited patiently for the finished product.

- Anglers: Malcolm Bell, Peter Francis, Ian McDonald, Franziska Wieland, Richard Emslie, John Eichelsheim, Bert Robinson, Dean Macmillan, Warren Agnew, Alan Martindale
- Additional Photography: Malcolm Bell, Ross Fraser, Scott Fraser
- Knot diagrams by Errol McLeary, based on sketches by Ross Fraser
- Adventure Consultants: Bill Lavelle, Scott Fraser, Brett Bowie
- Accommodation & Helicopters: Nokomai Station

Time out from the busy work schedule.

'Wherever the trout are,
it's beautiful.'

Thomas Masaryck

INTRODUCTION

New Zealand is a land blessed with fantastic trout fishing. Trophy brown and rainbow trout in excess of the magic 4.5 kg (10 lb.) mark can be targeted on a huge range of water from dainty gin-clear creeks to large, ominously deep lakes. For competent fly-fishing enthusiasts it is not unreasonable to expect to land 10 or more fish in a day on some waters, and this accomplishment would barely raise an eyebrow among many local anglers who know their home turf intimately. You could fish a different lake or river every day for a year and have just started on the available waters, which include glacier-fed braided rivers, shallow weedy lakes, clear spring creeks through to deep lakes formed in volcanic craters.

Destination Trout New Zealand started life from a conversation about the fact that New Zealand's trout fishing is so diverse, and that many anglers fishing these waters for the first time face a daunting task of where and when to fish. Some great fishing spots you can park right next to, whereas others require serious hiking or helicopters to access them. Some of the fisheries are best in the middle of the day in the height of summer, while others are best fished on frosty winter nights. Another issue was how best to showcase the scenic beauty and timeless allure of a selection of our many hundreds of trout-fishing destinations.

The conversation led to an expansive project, which at times became an epic adventure as we toured the country from one fly-fishing nirvana to the next. We also constantly grappled with how best to create a work that would be universally appealing to fly anglers around the globe. Looking back, it seems hard to imagine that we managed to complete our mission at all, yet alone in under two years.

ABOVE: This trout will grow up to trophy size in two to three years.

This book is by no means a comprehensive guide to all the trout waters available. We have focused our attention on only a dozen locations; some are dealt with intimately and a few are covered on a broader regional basis. However, we feel it offers anglers a true sampling of New Zealand's unique and diverse range of trout-fishing waters and to our knowledge this is the most comprehensive fly-fishing travelogue attempted in New Zealand.

The aim of the dual resources of book and DVD is to enable anglers from across the globe to experience the real action, sights and sounds in a multimedia format that is packed full of information and entertainment. The DVD volumes follow the layout of the book and cover

OPPOSITE: Big smile for a hard-won Tekapo rainbow.

A quick refuel before the adventure resumes.

all 12 destinations, allowing you to experience first hand the magnificent angling, the natural splendour and a taste of the many other adventures and activities available.

While the beautiful isles of New Zealand offer phenomenal fly-fishing opportunities, it would be an injustice to focus solely on the angling and not provide an insight into the many other activities and attractions each of these destinations has to offer travellers from both near and afar. We have been fortunate enough to travel, live and work in this magnificent environment. This has given us a traveller's perspective of the highlights far from the well-trodden tourist trails, and we feel this is far more interesting to fly anglers and visitors looking for a true Kiwi experience.

The thousands of hours we spent tramping the countryside with a collection of angling gear, broadcast cameras, still cameras, audio equipment, tripods and assorted paraphernalia has been a fantastic, at times comical, and constantly exciting odyssey that has proved thoroughly enlightening. We dearly hope that the book and DVD exude at least a fraction of our passion for fly fishing and the great outdoors of New Zealand.

Most of all, we would love to think that these resources inspire anglers and travellers as well as arming them with the practical information required to fish the locations and to successfully target trout in a wide diversity of environments, seasons and conditions regardless of where in the world they happen upon a trout.

TROUT FISHING IN NEW ZEALAND

Trout are amazingly adaptive creatures that have survived monumental changes to their environment over millennia. There are, in fact, many species and sub species worldwide that fall under the generic name 'trout' and these are spread across a very wide and diverse range of native habitats in the northern hemisphere. Over more recent centuries, trout have been introduced to the far corners of the earth by homesick anglers and explorers.

Many keen fly fishers would not associate exotic locations such as the Euphrates River, Morocco, Lebanon, Mongolia or the Balkans as the homes of indigenous trout species, but varieties of these most popular of sport fish exist from North America and Europe to Asia and North Africa.

There are no native trout in the southern hemisphere. All New Zealand's trout species are introduced but now ironically (in the case of rainbow trout and brown trout) we have some of the healthiest remaining wild populations on earth. It is alarming with what ease native fish populations can be destroyed by man. Many unique varieties around the globe are now extinct including the native New Zealand grayling trout, upokororo (*Prototroctes oxyrhynchus*) and others like the giant brown trout of the Caspian Sea, which once reached weights over 45kgs (100 lb.) but have now been decimated to the brink of extinction.

> '*If fishing is a religion, fly fishing is the high church.*'
> Tom Brokaw

Kent in North West Mongolia about to release a Mongolian Taimen (Hucho taimen), an ancestral relative of trout and salmon.

Brown Trout (*Salmo trutta*)

Shipments of brown trout ova in the 19th century were shipped from England to Tasmania and the first recorded transfer to New Zealand was in the early 1860s, although it is believed that these first attempts were unsuccessful. Shipments of ova were imported to the South Island in 1867 and 1868, so it is generally accepted that by 1868 brown trout were established in New Zealand.

Rainbow Trout (*Salmo gairdnerii*)

OPPOSITE TOP: Bert Robinson from Fish and Game measuring fish at the Ngongotaha Trap.

OPPOSITE BOTTOM: Kids' fishing day at the Ngongotaha Hatchery, Rotorua.

BELOW: The prime condition of this silver-flanked Kiwi rainbow is testament to the steelhead ancestry.

The first rainbow trout introduced to New Zealand came from their native home in North America. The exact origin of the first shipment of ova has however been a source of much debate. It seems likely that the first successful importation of ova was in 1883 and that these eggs came from 'Steelhead' rainbows that spawned in rivers that flow to the sea and actually lived in the sea for part of their lives. The likely origin of the New Zealand rainbows is from Sonoma Creek, a tributary stream that empties into San Francisco Bay. These eggs were successfully reared in ponds at the Auckland domain from where the species was eventually released throughout New Zealand.

Brook Trout (*Salvelinus fontinalis*)

This species is actually a member of the char family and has not fared well where it has been released in waters shared with other species like rainbow and brown trout.

There are a few isolated pockets of brook trout in both the North and South Island, but anglers rarely target them.

Other introduced freshwater species available to fly fishers include quinnat salmon (*Onchorhynchus tschawytcha*), Atlantic salmon (*Salmo salar*), sockeye salmon (*Oncorhynchus nerka*) and MacKinaw trout (*Salvelinus namaycush*).

There are no trout farms in New Zealand as the commercial breeding and raising of trout is prohibited. The majority of trout waters in New Zealand are managed by the New Zealand Fish and Game Council, which offers a single licence for all 12 of their regions across the country. The main exception is the Lake Taupo District which is managed separately by the Department of Conservation (DOC) and requires a separate licence. With a Fish and Game licence and a Taupo licence, anglers have access to more water than they could hope to fish in a lifetime. Thanks to these agencies, the work of many volunteers, the cooperation of anglers and the stewardship of all New Zealanders, the country offers the best wild-trout fishery in the world. At the time of writing, the total cost of the two full-season licences was less than NZ$160.00, which is arguably the best-value fly fishing in the world and significantly below the daily rate charged in some countries. There is no excuse for not having a licence and all anglers should be aware that the modest fee is put to good use in maintaining and protecting the fishery.

In addition to the licence you need to check the relevant local regulations for the water you are about to fish. These stipulate open seasons, permitted fishing methods, bag and size limits and other important restrictions that need to be observed. The regulations mentioned in this book are current at the time of printing. Be aware

that regulations change from season to season, so take the time to read the relevant regulations for your water. Some of the fisheries are wild and self-sustaining while others are a blend of wild and stocked fish. A visit to a hatchery is always interesting and worth the effort to get a more in-depth look at the resource New Zealand has to offer. Finally, a little anecdote about trout fishing in New Zealand. On our first day of research (we call it research, others call it fishing) in our first hour of fishing, we landed four fish; the largest weighed around the respectable 5kg (11 lb.) mark and the smallest around 3kg (7 lb.). We sat back congratulating ourselves and basked in a warm glow of confidence. Of course, the very next day on the same water we caught nothing. Fly fishing in New Zealand can be like that, although the good days far outweigh the fishless ones – and when you stop staring at your fly drifting down the river and take in the magnificence of your surroundings, there is rarely a bad day on the water.

WEIGHTS AND MEASURES

New Zealand uses the metric system for weights and measures, but as a legacy of our history as an outpost of the British Empire the Imperial system is also still frequently used, especially by anglers when bragging about fish weights – after all, pounds do seem to make them sound bigger.

For standardisation of this text we have incorporated both systems to keep everyone happy.

- kilograms (kg) to pounds (lb.): 1 kg is equivalent to 2.2 lb.
- centimetres (cm) to inches (in.): 2.5 cm is approximately 1 in.
- metres (m) to feet (ft.): 1 metre is approximately 3.3 feet.
- kilometres (km) to miles (miles): 1 km is equivalent to 0.6 miles.
- Celsius (ºC) to Fahrenheit (ºF): multiply by 9, divide by 5, and add 32.

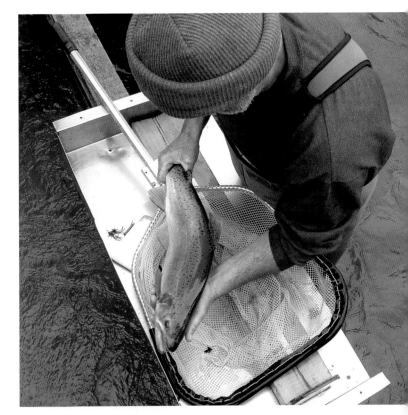

'The man who coined the phrase "Money can't buy happiness" never bought himself a good fly rod!'

Reg Baird

EQUIPMENT AND APPAREL

I t is said that success is 90 per cent preparation and 10 per cent luck, and as far as any fly-fishing trip goes this is true. The simplest detail can really make the difference between success and failure. It could be carrying nymphs with enough weight in the body to get down in a deep clear pool, using a leader system that can roll out a large fly in the face of a strong wind, or even having clothes that are comfortable enough so that you can fish hard all day and be ready when you come across that trophy fish.

The equipment listed below is a guide based on the most suitable in general terms for the areas and conditions that are likely to be encountered. Our fishing approach requires us to use very functional and durable equipment that will perform and keep on performing season after

season. All our terminal tackle, like hooks, leader material and braided loops are top quality and used in systems that have been tried and tested on literally thousands of fish. If you have these fundamentals covered, you will be well armed for any fly-fishing experience.

Equipment
Rods

Two rods will cover just about any conditions you are likely to encounter in New Zealand. For big water and lake fishing, a 2.75–2.9 m (9–9 ft. 6 in.) #9 weight rod is ideal as it gives you the ability to punch a line with a large wet fly or weighted nymph a long distance, and the muscle to prevent a good fish from running the rapids in big water. A graphite three-piece is the ideal travel rod.

OPPOSITE: A smile befitting for the 'Big O' – Lake Otamangakau.

LEFT: Although light, the #6 weight rod has plenty of power to handle trophy-sized fish.

ABOVE: A little time spent preparing the right equipment will pay dividends.

Rod tube

All rods should be transported in a crush-resistant rod tube. The simplest can be made from PVC plumbing pipe, and there are also plenty of good models available in tackle stores. Nothing will sour a trip faster than a broken rod.

Reels

A quality fly reel has three main attributes. Firstly, it must balance with the rod in order for the outfit to cast correctly; secondly, the drag must be smooth and progressive, and finally, it must have the capacity to hold a weight-forward floating fly line and 100 m (109 yards) of backing. In recent years the trend is to use large arbour reels as they retrieve more line per turn, which means you can keep your line tight on a fish that charges for freedom. The other advantage of the large arbour is they put larger loops in the fly line, which reduces tight memory coils.

A high-quality fly reel should last a lifetime, so it is worth investing some time and research into choosing the right one. Mid-price reels are generally good performers; reels in the lower range are inconsistent in their performance and tend to wear quickly with the frames often bending under pressure. Remember when purchasing reels to get at least two spare spools for additional fly lines.

Finer points to look for are large heavy-duty guides or snake rings, as many New Zealand rivers and lakes have fine grit or pumice that will wear out substandard guides quickly. A comfortable cork grip helps when casting all day; make sure it suits your hand size. The wince fitting or reel seat should accommodate your reel comfortably and make sure the locking rings fit snugly as there is nothing worse than tightening them all day or having a reel drop off during a fight.

The second rod recommendation is a 2.6 to 2.75 m (8 ft. 6 in. to 9 ft.) #6 weight rod. A three- or four-piece rod is ideal for the adventurous angler and will fit onto a small day pack with ease. This rod will serve mainly for dry-fly and nymph fishing. Stay away from slow-action rods; try to get one with a medium to quick action. These are ideal for short-range presentations where you need to cover a fish quickly and accurately. A good test is whether you can put a fly in a bucket consistently at 15 m (50 ft.) without splashing the water over the rim. Once again, the rod should ideally be graphite based and have good quality fittings.

Backing

For New Zealand conditions, reels should hold at least 100 m (109 yards) of backing. Use low-stretch Dacron or specialist fly-line backing as this is soft, rot resistant and will last for years. Backing serves two main purposes: it gives fly lines a bedding to lie on; and when a hard running fish takes out all your fly line, backing is your insurance policy against being spooled (losing all your line and usually the fish as well).

Fly lines

While there are a multitude of brands and styles of fly lines, of which anglers all have their own preferences, there are three basic lines that will cover just about every option for New Zealand conditions:

Floating line

A weight-forward floating line is a must. This line is ideal for dry-fly, nymphing, wet-fly fishing and shallow-water lure fishing. The line should have a medium-length head and float high in the water. A lot of river fishing in New Zealand involves mending the line constantly to remove drag from the flies, so ensure the belly or running line part of the line is not too thin as this can make mending difficult.

A useful tip for maintaining the floating properties of fly lines is to polish lines rather than use floatants. The sand and pumice in New Zealand rivers and lakes tends to stick to floatants, making lines dirty and causing them to waterlog and sink.

Intermediate lines

For controlled depth fishing in still and slow-moving waters the clear intermediate lines are a good choice. Get one that sinks at about 30 cm (12 in.) per five seconds. These lines are great for fishing big lures and wet flies over weed banks, drop-offs and river mouths; they can also be used for shoreline stalking with swimming nymph patterns and for smelt fishing where you want the fly just below the surface. The other advantage of the clear intermediate line is that you can use fairly short leaders without frightening fish.

Fast-sinking line

When you want to get flies down quickly or fish in deep, fast-flowing water, the best choice is an extra-fast sinking line in either weight-forward or shooting-head styles. Shooting-heads are good but may require the use of a stripping basket and the casting style required is also different to that used with a standard line. A weight-forward high-speed, high-density line will also work fine.

Tippets and leader materials

Attached to the end of the fly line is a leader or tippet, which can be made up of one length of line or constructed using several sections. The two materials we use are nylon monofilament and fluorocarbon monofilament. Fluorocarbon is far more expensive but supposedly has light refraction properties that make it less visible to fish and does, from our experience, outperform nylon monofilament in some conditions. You should carry breaking strains from 2 to 5 kg (4.4 to 11 lb.).

Tapered leaders are thicker at the butt than at the tip, making them capable of turning flies over in a straight and delicate presentation. They can be anywhere from 2 to 8 m long. Poly leaders are an extension to fly lines that when combined with a tapered leader and some fluorocarbon tippet make it possible to delicately roll out a 4 to 5 m (13 to 16 ft.) leader with large dry flies into a strong wind.

Apparel
Waders

Fly fishing is a year-round activity so wader options need to be considered carefully. For winter fishing, a pair of 5 to 7 mm (approximately one-fifth of an inch) neoprene waders is a must as water temperatures can be very cold. The drawback with these waders is that they are not easy to walk around in and can get unpleasantly hot and sweaty. However, if you are planning any winter or spring fishing, you will be thankful for the warmth and comfort these waders provide.

For fishing in milder conditions, a pair of good-quality breathable waders are a good choice. Use the stocking-foot variety with separate boots with felt soles, spikes or some other form of grip. The main drawback with breathable waders is they can be easily damaged in rough terrain.

In the heat of summer and especially when walking some distance, wet wading is a practical and very popular alternative. The standard Kiwi outfit is a pair of good thick polypropylene long johns with some fast-drying pants (shorts

ABOVE: Forceps are the best way to remove hooks efficiently.

ABOVE RIGHT: Quality Polaroid sunglasses are an essential piece of equipment.

or trousers) and a pair of tramping boots. Wet wading gives anglers the freedom to move around. The clothing is very comfortable, quick drying and provides protection from biting insects.

Fly vest items

Whether you wear a fly vest or carry a small pack, having the right accessories will help your fishing. Suggested items include:

- Fly floatants are an essential part of the fly fisher's arsenal and will keep a dry fly floating and looking good for hours. Occasionally, it is necessary to sink the leader, which is best done with a little detergent and fuller's earth mixture (obtainable from any pharmacy).
- Line clippers attached to an extendable lanyard are a fantastic tool.
- Forceps for removing hooks, also attached to a lanyard.
- A good-quality landing net. Make sure the hoop is big enough to hold a 4.5 kg (10 lb.) fish and that the mesh won't damage the scales.
- A small pocket knife or multi-tool.

- Three fly boxes: one for dry flies, another for nymphs and the third for wet flies and streamers.
- Insect repellent is definitely necessary.
- Sunblock is also a must. Use Sun Protection Factor (SPF) 15 or higher rating and use lip-protection sunblock too. The ultra violet rays in New Zealand are some of the strongest in the world so it is very important to use all forms of sun protection; nothing will spoil a trip like a bad dose of sunburn.

Polarised sunglasses

Polarised sunglasses are essential to reduce glare coming off the water, making spotting fish easier, and protecting your eyes from the sun and flies. Carry two pairs of good-quality polarised sunglasses. Make sure they fit well; wrap around models are a good choice as they keep out angled light. Lightweight plastic frames are preferable as you may be wearing the glasses all day. Make sure they are anti-fog or treat them with an anti-fog solution, and carry a micro-fibre cleaning cloth and hard case. Different waters and light conditions may require a selection of different-coloured lenses. Our first choice for New Zealand conditions is amber followed by copper.

Clothing

Most outdoor enthusiasts understand the concept of layering clothing. In New Zealand conditions this is particularly important due to the extremes of weather you can encounter. A good base is polypropylene thermal underwear consisting of long johns and a long-sleeve vest, fast-drying nylon trousers with zip-off legs to make shorts, and a long-sleeve vented shirt (materials with extra sun-protection are a recent innovation). Over this you can wear a polar-fleece sweatshirt and, to top the whole lot off, pack a waterproof breathable jacket that acts as a windbreak and keeps you dry.

The benefits of this system are that the whole ensemble is very lightweight and compact to carry if not being worn, it can be washed and dried quickly and layers can be swiftly added or removed to suit the conditions. It is all very soft and comfortable to wear and will not chaff or rub. If conditions are extreme, this clothing will help prevent hypothermia and could even save your life.

Finally, and very importantly, a suitable hat for the conditions. A good hat reduces glare, protects the face from elements and helps retain body heat. Don't worry about your fashion sense, the fish won't notice, in fact, bad taste and unusual hats seem to be quite the norm with Kiwi anglers. We have a few old faithfuls that seem to bring us luck and the odd remark. Wide-brimmed hats are great for sun protection in summer, while a peaked cap will suffice in the cooler months. For winter weather and night fishing, a cosy wool or polar fleece hat, which covers your ears, will conserve a lot of body heat.

Always dress for the conditions and remember weather can change abruptly in New Zealand.

'There's a fine line between fishing and standing on the shore like an idiot.'
Steven Wright

KNOTS, RIGS AND LEADERS

Knots

Our key philosophy with knots and leader systems is to keep it simple! You need only a handful of connecting knots to create all of your fly-fishing terminal rigs. If you can master the five knots illustrated below, you will have an excellent base to cover any situation. Learn to tie these quickly and proficiently so you gain the confidence to be able to regularly adjust or change your system throughout your fishing session. If you venture out in all seasons, remember that you will often be rigging in unfavourable conditions. The art of quickly tying precision knots in fine monofilament line becomes a real challenge in low light or darkness or when your fingers freeze up in the middle of winter.

We have permanent braided loops attached to the ends of all fly lines and recommend this as a great starting point for your terminal tackle system. End loops allow you to quickly change leaders, attach indicators or add an extra section of fly line. (We often connect a small section of sinking line to our floating lines to create a sinking tip.) By creating a simple small figure-of-eight loop in the butt section of your leader you can create a loop-to-loop connection between fly line and leader.

1. **Figure-of-eight loop** and the loop-to-loop connection: Keeping it simple, this combination is used to connect fly line to leader.

2. **Blood knot:** used to join two similar-sized lengths of monofilament. Reasonably easy to tie and retains good strength. This is the knot we use to create tapered leaders and attach tippets to leaders; it can also be easily modified to create a dropper by leaving one tag end untrimmed. When using dropper-style rigs for

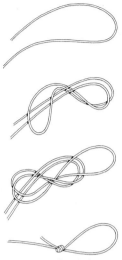

Figure-of-eight loop   **Loop-to-loop connection**

multiple fly presentation, keep the dropper length under 20 cm (8 in.) to avoid tangling. It is not suitable for joining lines with a significant difference in diameters.

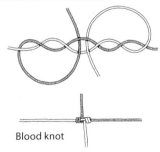

Blood knot

3. **Surgeon's knot:** A very easy knot to tie quickly and can be used as a substitute for the blood knot for building both leader and droppers. We use this knot to create droppers, as with the blood knot you need to leave an overlapping tag end for the dropper.

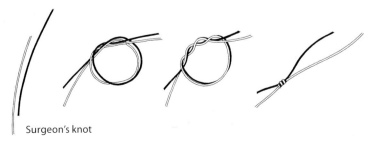

Surgeon's knot

4. **Indicator knot:** A great knot for attaching a piece of yarn or wool directly into your leader to act as a strike indicator. The benefit of this knot is that you can add an indicator at any point along the leader and you can remove or adjust the position of the indicator by loosening the knot.

5. **Uni knot:** A popular knot for attaching line to terminal tackle in all types of fishing. This is a simple knot to construct, it should not slip and it has one of the strongest knot strengths, breaking only fractionally under the line strength.

Indicator knot

Uni knot

Rigs

Here are a few of our favourite rigs and leader systems which we talk about in the various destination chapters of this book. All have various applications and the trick is to apply the right system for a given situation. Often more than one approach will work depending on the mood of your opponent and the skill of the angler. Leaders are important and worth spending time on fine tuning; an adjustment of a few centimetres or using a finer tippet can mean the difference between frustration and victory!

Tips and hints for tapered leaders ▼
- Tapered leaders are ideal for delicate presentation and optimal rollover of the leader when casting into the wind.
- Ensure that line diameters are similar when constructing manually tied leaders to prevent blood knots slipping.
- If you don't have time to hand-tie leaders then use one of the one-piece tapered leaders available in tackle stores.

To achieve an effective hand-tied leader use either the Ritz formula (for accurate straight layout even in windy conditions) or the Harvey formula (for layouts in soft curves for delicate presentation and drag-free drift). Be aware that different monofilaments have different stiffness and diameter properties. These formulae work well when tied with Maxima material.

The Ritz Formula (All hard Maxima material)		The Harvey Formula (Hard and soft Maxima)	
Length (cm)	Diameter	Length (m)	Diameter
100	.018	25	.017 (Hard)
90	.016	50	.015 (Hard)
15	.014	50	.013 (Hard)
15	.010	30	.011 (Soft)
15	.009	45	.009 (Soft)
15	.008	60	.007 (Soft)
62	.007		

Long tapered leaders (9 ft. to 20 ft.)
For dry fly and nymph presentation.

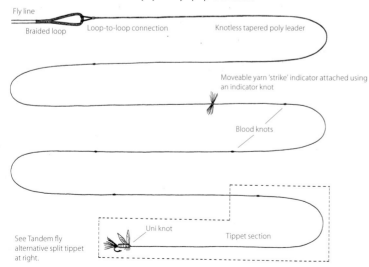

Fly line

Braided loop

Loop-to-loop connection

Knotless tapered poly leader

Moveable yarn 'strike' indicator attached using an indicator knot

Blood knots

See Tandem fly alternative split tippet at right.

Uni knot

Tippet section

Tandem fly alternative split tippet (dropper rig)
For fishing two fly combinations, for example two dry flies, dry and emerger pattern, two nymphs or dry fly and nymph.

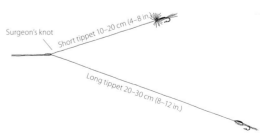

Surgeon's knot

Short tippet 10–20 cm (4–8 in.)

Long tippet 20–30 cm (8–12 in.)

Tongariro-style nymphing rig

For swift, deep rivers where heavily weighted nymphs ('bombs') are required to reach fish hard on the bottom. Suited to larger flylines of 8 to 10 weight and rods of 9–11 ft. A yarn indicator treated for buoyancy is attached to the flyline loop and needs to be large enough to remain afloat against the pull of weighted nymphs and river currents.

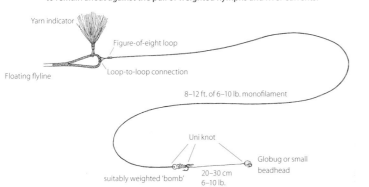

Yarn indicator

Figure-of-eight loop

Floating flyline

Loop-to-loop connection

8–12 ft. of 6–10 lb. monofilament

Uni knot

suitably weighted 'bomb'

20–30 cm
6–10 lb.

Globug or small
beadhead

◄ Tips and hints

Estimate the average depth of the water you are about to explore. Make your leader roughly 25per cent longer than the depth, e.g., if the water is 8 ft. deep use a 10 ft. leader. Tungsten is heavier than lead and therefore you can use a smaller faster sinking 'bomb'. In clear water conditions, use small natural nymphs as the point fly.

Tips and hints ►

- Use high density foam to give fly buoyancy to keep it hovering above the bottom. The deeper the water the more flotation to counter water pressure.
- On weedless bottoms a very short leader of 2–3 ft. can be more effective.
- Alter the retrieve from a very slow knit to short sharp tugs to long draws with a pause. This method can also be very effective with flies fished static with no retrieve at all.

Deep-water lake rig

Short leaders used to keep buoyant flies close to the lake bed.

Hi-density shooting-head
fly line.

2–6 ft. of 6–10 lb. monofilament

Booby, floating snail or Globug

Evening and night-time rigs

Used on lakes, streams and rivers with both floating and sinking lines to present a wide variety of dry flies, nymphs and wet flies.

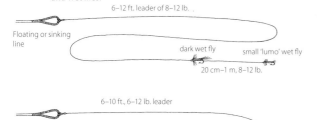

6–12 ft. leader of 8–12 lb.

Floating or sinking
line

dark wet fly

small 'lumo' wet fly

20 cm–1 m, 8–12 lb.

6–10 ft., 6–12 lb. leader

Floating line

dry fly

wet fly, nymph, emerger or second dry fly

30 cm–1.5 m

◄ Tips and hints

If there is a breeze or you are experiencing tangles then switch to a single fly rig. Use a torch or camera flash to get your lumo flies glowing.

◄ Tips and hints

Try fishing these combinations across and downstream in an arc. Keep the rod high to accentuate skittering of dry flies across the surface film and to detect sudden grabs. Ensure dry flies are well floated by regularly dressing with floatant.

Tips and Hints ►

- As a general rule, use shorter leader lengths when fishing swifter, deeper sections of river. Short leaders keep the flies fluttering in the strike zone close to the bottom. This style of river fishing is effective day and night and has secured a number of large brown trout for us over the years.
- Try a tandem rig, but keep the point fly smaller and within 40 cm of the lead fly to avoid tangles. With shooting-head lines a stripping basket can be very useful to prevent the shooting line catching the ground or being pulled away by the current.

Fast sinking wet line rig

For traditional salmon style across and downstream fishing.

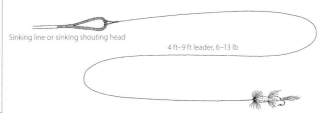

Sinking line or sinking shouting head

4 ft–9 ft leader, 6–13 lb

'When I was young, I danced with nymphs. Now I only fish them.'
Jimmy D. Moore

TROUT FLIES

For over 5000 years, anglers across the globe from various cultures have designed a countless array of flies from every imaginable material, with the single-minded purpose of enticing the elusive trout. Old patterns vanish and new creations appear at an astonishing rate. There is an unimaginable range of patterns in all shapes, colours, sizes and styles. At the fly-tying vice science, fantasy and art are fused together like magic and the creator's imagination can run wild.

Many years ago I inherited my grandfather's fly collection, which was stored haphazardly in ancient rusty tobacco tins. There were literally hundreds of flies, most of which my grandmother assured me had caught trout, but, interestingly, very few resemble any conventional pattern I have ever encountered. I still open the battered old tins from time to time for inspiration; they are a reminder that tying is truly an artistic pursuit. Whether tied to specifically imitate a natural organism or just tied on a whim, they will all work in the right place at the right time with a good cast and a sprinkle of luck.

Trout have adapted to a wide range of habitats around the world. They are highly opportunist feeders and will eat anything from small rodents to the tiniest insect. They can also be cannibalistic: on several occasions I have witnessed anglers hooked into fingerlings only to have these attacked and sometimes devoured by large brown trout.

We have our favourite patterns, which we fish with confidence, but the reality is that many patterns would be equally successful in most situations. Try to be receptive to new styles, patterns and inventions; there is no finite number of killer patterns.

ABOVE: Traditional wet flies used to good effect in New Zealand waters in yesteryear.

OPPOSITE AND LEFT: Fly creations are only limited by your imagination

As keen fly tiers, we often alter existing styles to create a more lifelike lure. Many commercial flies tend to be overdressed and unbalanced in their bodies, causing them to swim unnaturally. Take time and care when buying flies to avoid disappointment.

The flies we have selected for each location are a guide only and you should not limit yourself to this selection. Many overseas flies not

The killer Glo Bug, an introduced pattern from the USA.

Cicadas are a favourite terrestrial food for New Zealand trout.

common in New Zealand can work superbly on our trout; examples are the North American glow bug flies, which have made an impact on the Tongariro rainbow fishery, or the British reservoir booby patterns. Of greater importance than any individual fly is stocking a good selection of styles, patterns, sizes and weights. There is a huge variety of terrestrial and aquatic food sources available to New Zealand trout. Rather than selecting randomly from your collection, try to match the obvious or likely food source, whether it is mice or cicadas on the surface or bloodworms and caddis from the bottom. Selecting the right fly is always a chancy affair and confidence from experience and a willingness to experiment will increase your success. Size and presentation is very often more critical than the pattern or colour.

Styles of Flies
Dry flies

Dry flies, aided by the hackles and tail, are dressed to float on the surface. They represent adult flies such as mayflies, caddis-flies, damselflies, stone-flies, midges as well as terrestrials like cicadas and beetles. Apply floatant to your flies to ensure they sit in the correct layer of water. For fast, rough water a large visible fly, well-hackled or incorporating hair, should float high on the surface film where flies hatch and take off. Lighter dressings may be more appropriate for slower water where flies are just hatching or emerging. We often fish another dry, wet fly or nymph behind our leading dry fly to cover more options.

Nymphs

Nymphs are usually dressed in an attempt to mimic subaquatic insects. 'Nymph' is a generic term covering a wide range of larvae, grubs, crustaceans and pupae. Your selection of nymphs should range in weight so that various depths can be explored. Unweighted nymphs can sit just below the surface, while heavily weighted nymphs will bounce along the bottom in fast, deep water. A tandem rig of nymphs allows two distinctly different patterns and sizes.

Wet flies

Wet flies are also referred to as 'winged wets' or 'soft hackle flies'. These imitations can be lethal when fished either individually or as a team on floating or sinking lines. In general, they are under-utilised by Kiwi anglers. They are designed to resemble emerging and hatching flies and small baitfish. Wet flies are an excellent choice at sunset or in darkness when fish breaking the surface are ignoring dry flies.

Streamer/lure

The streamer or lure is a large-scale wet fly, often used as an 'attractor' or 'imitation' of baitfish, crayfish or young trout. They are very effective on sea trout and for night fishing. Try fishing these on sinking or fast-sinking lines across and downstream in salmon style on rivers or stream, or a slow-to-medium-pace retrieve in still water. The Booby Fly, a floating variation incorporating Styrofoam, is an import from the United Kingdom and has become very popular for lake fishing. It is used on a short leader with a high-density line so the flies hover enticingly above the bottom, mimicking smelt, snails and koura (freshwater crayfish).

LEFT (TOP): The silhouette of an Adams dry fly offers a tantalising imitation of the real thing.

LEFT (BELOW): Weighted bead-head nymphs.

Twilight Beauty.

Woolly Bugger streamer fly.

Black Rabbit streamer fly.

A WORD ABOUT SAFETY

New Zealand offers wonderful opportunities for a wide range of recreational pursuits and wilderness experiences. Fly fishing is one of many enjoyable activities where the individual can escape the pressures of everyday life and seek solitude, freedom and independence by living closer to nature. But before you set off on the adventure remember that this freedom entails responsibilities for yourself, for others and for the environment.

Many great angling spots can be reached a short distance from your vehicle while others can be extremely remote and very difficult to access. Be aware that no matter where the location, there will always be hazards and associated risks. If you are not experienced in back-country fishing then go with someone who is. There are many professional guides in New Zealand (NZ Professional Fishing Guides Association, www.nzpfga.com) who can plan and manage anglers' adventures and ensure the enjoyment and safety of everyone. If you are planning a remote wilderness trip, you must carefully consider the consequences of going into the bush alone. Going alone requires you to accept even greater responsibilities for yourself and while this is a privilege that some enjoy, it is unwise for beginners.

Rivers and waterways present possibly the greatest hazard for all outdoor enthusiasts and it is an area that requires special mention for anglers who spend much of their time on the banks or in the water. Water-related deaths continue

LEFT: This angler is experienced in this section of river and knows her wading safety limit.

OPPOSITE: A calm summer day on Lake Hawea.

to be a tragic reality of the outdoor recreation scene in New Zealand and you need to be both aware of the variety of problems and sufficiently experienced before attempting activities such as wading or river crossings.

Risks include being swept away, being trapped by snags or whirlpools, and the risk of hypothermia from exposure to cold water. All rivers and waterways such as lakes and canals vary and there is no substitute for local knowledge, experience and caution. Treat all water with respect – 'If in doubt – don't cross'. If you choose to cross and have companions then use the mutual support of others, move diagonally across the river utilising the power of the current to help you across, and anticipate what might go wrong by carefully picking your spot to cross or wade to avoid hazards. Wading staffs are a good accessory for skilled anglers to brace themselves on slippery rocks or in difficult currents. If something goes wrong and you find yourself swept downstream, get your feet up on the surface and pointed

downstream as quickly as possible. Properly fitted waders or backpacks will provide natural buoyancy and by angling your drift diagonally across the current and using your arms and legs for propulsion you can move towards the nearest bank safely. Stay calm; as long as you are properly equipped and have chosen a good wading or crossing spot you should soon be swept towards a bank and be able to recover your footing.

Dehydration

On the other end of the scale from hypothermia, anglers need to protect themselves from the sun and overheating and dehydration. Heatstroke and heat exhaustion can become life threatening. It is essential to stay well hydrated when you are in the outdoors. If you are concerned about the quality or taste of the natural water supply, carry a water bottle. This will help keep you alert and concentration levels up for the important things like spotting fish.

RIGHT: Fish aren't the only creatures who need water.

PROTECT OUR WATERS

New Zealand has some of the most beautiful and fragile ecosystems and waterways in the world, free of many exotic pests both terrestrial and aquatic. To help keep our waterways that way we need your help to stop the spread of pests.

The recent discovery of the invasive alga *Didymosphenia geminata* (didymo) in several South Island waterways has highlighted the importance of good cleaning procedures between waterways to limit the spread of aquatic pests. Didymo can impact on what we all love most about our lakes and rivers – the fishing, kayaking or simply getting out and enjoying the scenery.

It is now a legal requirement to clean any items that have been in contact with lakes and rivers when leaving the South Island or before using them in another waterway.

This is not an impossible battle but it does require everyone, everywhere, every time to take responsibility to decontaminate all gear.

Check
Before leaving the waterway, remove all obvious debris from items that have been in contact with the water.
Clean
Soak and scrub all items for at least one minute in either hot (60°C) water, a two per cent solution of household bleach, or a five per cent solution of salt, dog shampoo, nappy cleaner, antiseptic hand cleaner or dishwashing detergent. A two per cent solution is 200 ml, a five per cent solution is 500 ml (two large cups), with water added to make 10 litres.
Dry
If cleaning is not practical, after the item is completely dry to touch wait an additional 48 hours before contact or use in any other waterway.
Our plea to everyone is to **CHECK, CLEAN, DRY!** It's that simple.

It's not hard! It is essential that all anglers and other river and lake users adopt **CHECK, CLEAN, DRY** as a matter of routine.

Before you use your equipment in any waterway clean it thoroughly using the methods indicated below. Then after using a waterway always check, clean, dry all items that have been in the water before using them in another waterway.

Young didymo algae colonies.

Stu Sutherland of Fish and Game NZ, showing the devastating effects of didymo on the Mararoa River. (Photo: Zane Moss)

'Rivers and the inhabitants of the watery elements are made for wise men to contemplate and for fools to pass by without consideration.'

Izaac Walton

OHINEMURI AND WAIHOU RIVERS

1

WAI (WATER); HOU (COLD OR NEW) – THE WAIHOU IS FED FROM COOL SPRINGS AND COULD ALSO BE CONSIDERED A NEW RIVER IN THE SENSE THAT IT HAS CUT NEW CHANNELS.

The hills around the Ohinemuri River are famous for the gold that was mined long ago and, much like those hills, the Ohinemuri has a few treasures to be discovered. Located a little over one and a half hours from Auckland, the Ohinemuri River flows through the Karangahake Gorge from Waihi to Paeroa where it joins the Waihou River. This delightful river features long gliding runs, boulder-strewn pocket water, deep pools and shallow riffles that all hold fish.

I rate the Ohinemuri as one of my favourite rivers because of the abundance and willingness of the 1 to 1.5 kg (2.2 to 3.3 lb.) rainbows to take a fly and the more elusive browns that are occasionally fooled by a well-presented offering. These browns do grow to good proportions and fish of over 2.5 kg (5 lb.) are caught regularly. This brown-trout stock is said to be sea run, with silver sided specimens occasionally caught in the brackish water of the lower Waihou a few kilometres downstream of the confluence with the Ohinemuri. There is anecdotal evidence of browns being caught at the local wharf at the nearby seaside town of Thames.

Another endearing feature of the Ohinemuri is being able to drive alongside the river through the gorge section and park right beside the river and to fish likely stretches of water. The trucks that tear past you on the road are soon out of earshot as the bush-clad river surrounds soak up the noise and you feel like you could be miles from anywhere. It is an ideal river to teach the art of fly fishing and is a great place to take a picnic and spend the day exploring. Most of the river is easy wading except for the lower reaches just before Paeroa, where the high overgrown banks can involve a

Hare and Copper – don't leave home without these superb flies. Try the most ragged and untidy specimens for best results.

LEFT: The road through the Karangahake Gorge winds along the Ohinemuri river.
OPPOSITE: Prime pocket water on the Ohinemuri.

bit of scrambling and deep wading. Although the Ohinemuri fishes well all year, the most exciting fishing is from November onwards when the surface activity increases. The river has a slight tannin colour, but fish can be spotted with relative ease in normal flow conditions. As the river runs through a gorge, it is prone to flooding but the levels fall quickly and the river becomes fishable after two or three days of heavy rainfall.

(See the river levels website in the Resources section on page 39.)

The Ohinemuri flows into the Waihou River, which is the main artery for many of the streams and rivers in this area. The lower reaches of the Waihou are not particularly attractive to fish but do hold a reasonable stock of both rainbow and brown trout. If you travel for about 40 minutes from Paeroa through Matamata on State Highway 27 to Okoroire, the Waihou transforms to a lovely watercress-lined spring creek that flows gently through farmland. There are good sized fish but this pretty section of the Waihou produces lots of small rainbows, which although entertaining can become a nuisance when searching for the larger specimens.

The Waihou is the type of river that you may spend a few hours or half a day on if you were travelling to Rotorua or Taupo, but you would probably not base a major trip on this water alone. However, the Waihou does have many tributaries and other streams nearby that can make for a good few days exploring in the region. There are some surprisingly good fish to be had in the lovely streams especially in early autumn when fish head upstream to spawn. If you approach these streams with light 1 to 2 kg (2.2 to 4 lb.) tippets, small flies and a #4 to #6 weight rod you will have great fishing and a 2 kg (4.4 lb.) fish would represent a real challenge. Access to most of these streams and the Waihou itself is through dairy farms so remember to ask the local farmers, who are normally very obliging.

TOP: Easy wading on the Ohinemuri, but take care during periods of heavy rain.

ABOVE: Tantalising spring-fed water on the upper Waihou.

RIGHT: This Waihou rainbow fell for a bead-head nymph.

Gearing up for a mission.

Getting There

To get to the Ohinemuri River from Auckland, take State Highway 2 to Paeroa then drive into the Karangahake Gorge, where the middle and lower sections of the river run alongside the road. For the more endearing upper and middle sections of the Waihou head along State Highway 5. A standard road map will help you a lot in this area.

Access

A great feature of many of the fishing spots in this region is they are very easy to access, being either in designated reserve areas or accessible through farmland. Many of the spots can be reached by parking on the side of the road and crossing a short stretch of grassland. It is essential to gain permission from the landowner if going onto private property. The walking is normally over gentle terrain and the rivers in the upper sections are easily crossed through the shallow runs. Other recommended streams in this vicinity include the Waiomou Stream – another tributary of the Waihou, the Kakahu and the Waimakiriri Streams.

Angling

The greatest challenge when fishing the Ohinemuri and Waihou is to stalk and catch one of the larger fish that inhabit these waterways. It is important to keep a low profile move slowly, and constantly scan the water for any holding fish. Quite often the larger fish will lie under the undercut banks or at the back of fallen trees or logs. These fish can be tempted out of their lairs to take a well-presented dry fly or nymph. Most of the year small caddis imitations work really well in both nymph and dry forms. During the warmer months, large dries – tied to imitate cicadas and crickets – can evoke surprisingly aggressive strikes. Willow grubs are also present in late summer and can be imitated by using a size 14 to 16 nymph in a yellow to light-green colour. Scaling down your tackle and keeping your leader long and light will help you get more strikes. In most places, indicators are not necessary as watching the leader will give enough notification of a strike.

FAR LEFT: Peter Francis about to release a dry fly-caught rainbow.

LEFT: Back to the river to grow for this pretty little rainbow.

Angler and camera awaiting the take!

Season

Ohinemuri: Open all year below Victoria Street Bridge and from 1 October to 30 June above Victoria Street Bridge. The bag limit is five trout with a minimum size of 30 cm (12 in.).

Waihou: Open all year. Below Okoroire there is a bag limit of five trout with a minimum size of 30 cm (12 in.). Above Okoroire there is no limit on small fish less than 30 cm (12 in.) but anglers may only keep two trout over 30 cm (12 in.).

Dry flies should be buoyant and easily visible.

Techniques and Tactics

For larger fish the early autumn period from March to May is a good time to explore middle and upper reaches of both rivers with nymphs and wet flies. But our favourite season to fish is summer time when the dry fly angling comes into its own.

Our preferred conditions are warm sunny days, and the less wind the better. The best hatches tend to be at change of light and into darkness, although you will still get random rising fish throughout the day.

It is interesting to note where fish tend to lie in these rivers. There are always the obvious spots like pools and behind large rocks. The challenge in these waters is that fish will lie in less obvious spots that you might have overlooked elsewhere. A classic lie on the Ohinemuri are the foamy side pockets away from the fast water, and on the Waihou look for fish in the gravel channels between weed banks.

If fishing upstream, nymph and dry flies work very well or use a combination of both. Some of the trickier water not suited to an upstream approach can be covered using a pair of small wet flies trickled downstream through likely looking water on an intermediate or slow-sinking line. The latter of these techniques is very good for targeting large fish that often lie in wait under cutaway banks. Having a companion acting as a spotter working from the opposite bank will help you locate fish that would otherwise remain unseen, and can also help direct you to approach a fish with minimal disturbance.

Flies and Rigs

The smaller patterns work best in the clear, slow waters, and anything that resembles a caddis will work fine. A lightly dressed Hare and Copper in sizes 12 to 16 is very consistent as is the Halfback in the same size. Dries in sizes 12 to 16 with upwing varieties in browns and greys like Dad's Favourite, Coch-y-Bondhu or Parachute Adams are all a safe bet. The water is very slow in some stretches so it can pay to dress leaders close to the fly so that the tippet sinks, casting less shadow and looking more natural. Unless there is a hatch in progress, it may be necessary to change rigs to suit each piece of water. The shallower water can be covered with a dry fly and small nymph trailing on a dropper, up to half a metre (20 in.) long. In the deeper pools it is always a good idea to probe around with a small bead-head nymph and weighted Hare and Copper on a 2.7 m (9 ft.) leader with a small yarn indicator attached with an indicator-knot so you can slide it up and down the leader to suit the varying depths.

Tips and Tricks

Even if you can't see any obvious sign of fish, cover the water methodically by casting to all likely looking spots, especially the shallow runs. If you see a fish feeding, take the time to set up your approach. Look at how the drift will affect your presentation. Amber-coloured Polaroid glasses will give the best penetration in the tannin-coloured water of the Ohinemuri.

Carry a good selection of nymphs and dry flies.

John Eichelsheim gets into a fish on the nymph.

Wear drab-coloured clothing and avoid anything that may flash and thus disturb the fish.

We didn't spend too much time blind fishing any particular spot. Depending on the time of the year, the fish in these systems can be spread quite some distance apart and it pays to take a mobile approach and cover plenty of mileage.

Flora and Fauna

Like much of New Zealand, the Ohinemuri and Waihou Rivers flow through varying landscapes such as the Karangahake Gorge, located where the Ohinemuri cuts its path through the Coromandel Ranges to join the Waihou River. The region is densely covered in native bush as well as introduced plants like blackberry and gorse. Many native birds are regularly sighted or heard throughout this area. The New Zealand native pigeon or kereru is a large bird with greyish green feathers on its back and head, and a smart white vest. The pattern of its wings in flight and distinctive beat make the native pigeon easy to identify as does its large size compared to the common pigeon. The tui, another native bird, has a prominent white tuft at the throat and a white patch on the wing. They are usually dark black with variable metallic blue-green colouring. The unique song of the tui often rings out through the bush. The Tui is attracted by flowering trees and has a special fondness for the nectar of the kowhai tree and flax bush. The little fantail or piwakawaka bird is a delight and a frequent bush companion; it has little fear of humans and will often fly quite close to catch insects disturbed as one walks through bush.

The Waihou flows mainly through the pastoral land of the Hauraki Plains down to the sea. Small stands of poplar and pines are growing with willows, planted as wind breaks and to prevent erosion along the banks. Many species of water fowl are common with the pukeko – a species of marsh hen, with a purple-black colouration and a red beak and comb – being one of the most prolific. On warm summer days the song of the skylark, a species that that was introduced to New Zealand from Europe in the 1860s, will serenade anglers all day.

Filming takes as much patience as fishing!

THINGS TO REMEMBER

DO:

- Drive carefully through the gorge. It is easy to forget you are on a main highway when you are surveying the river for likely spots.
- Check the river conditions when planning a trip.
- Move up and down the river until you find where the fish are holding.
- Take insect repellent, sunscreen and food.
- Keep a low profile.
- Take a good selection of fly sizes, eights and patterns (size 10–16).

DON'T:

- Overlook small pockets of water.
- Wade unless necessary. It is very easy to spook fish in the shallows.
- Discard trace line or rubbish.
- Disturb livestock.
- Enter private property without permission.

THINGS TO DO

Paeroa is a small township based around the farming and agriculture of the area. Gold-mining was once a significant feature of this region and the surrounding hills still have vast reserves of gold. Although there are a few active mines, mining has mostly given way to conservation of this magnificent region.

Visit the Lemon and Paeroa Bottle and discover the history of the local mineral waters used for their health-giving properties. and how they developed into one of New Zealand's most popular soft drinks. The Visitor Centre has displays featuring the gold mining and timber history of the general area, as well as information on walks and other facilities in nearby parks and reserves.

- Action and Adventure: Gold panning, mountain biking, bush walking, hiking, horse trekking, wild pig and duck hunting.
- Eco and Nature: Tramping, eco-tours, farm stays, bird watching.
- Health and Relaxation: Thermal pools, walks, golf.
- Arts and Gardens: Galleries, jewelry, crafts, rural arts.

- Shows and Events: Agricultural and pastoral shows.
- Food and Wine: Ohinemuri Estate has a vineyard, restaurant and limited accommodation.
  Moresby Street, Karangahake
  RD 4, New Zealand
  Ph: +64-7-862 8874
  Fax: +64-7-862 8847
  www.ohinemuri.co.nz

Maps

A good road map will suffice for this destination but for more detail obtain Topographical Map 260-T13 (Paeroa).

Resources

Paeroa Visitor Centre
1 Belmont Street
Ph: +64-7-862 8636
Fax: +64-7-862 8636
Email: lesley.w@xtra.co.nz

Matamata iSite Visitor Information Centre
45 Broadway
Matamata
Ph: +64-7-888 7260
Email: info@matamatanz.co.nz

www.fishandgame.org
Useful for maps, downloadable brochures and fishing regulations for each region (key words: Ohinemuri, Waihou).

Water levels

A useful site for checking the levels of the Ohinemuri River: www.ew.govt.nz/enviroinfo/riverlevelsandrainfall/riverlevelsmap

Rangiuru Bay – Lake Tarawera.

'Scholars have long known that fishing
eventually turns men into philosophers.
Unfortunately, it is almost impossible to
buy decent tackle on a philosopher's salary.'
Patrick F. McManus

ROTORUA LAKES DISTRICT

2

ROTO (LAKE); RUA (TWO) – THE FULL NAME WAS ROTORUA-NUI-A-KAHU. LAKE ROTORUA WAS THE
SECOND BIG LAKE DISCOVERED BY IHENGA, WHO NAMED IT AFTER HIS FATHER-IN-LAW KAHU-MATA-MOMOE.

Any trip to New Zealand would be incomplete without experiencing some of what the Rotorua Lakes District has to offer. In fact, if you had only a short time to fish this would definitely be one of the best places to base yourself in the North Island. What makes Rotorua unique – apart from its bubbling mud pools, sulphurous smell and geothermal wonderlands – is the sheer diversity of fishing options available. You could choose to fish a small crystal clear stream that flows through massive forest using dry fly in the heat of summer or target large trophy trout in the dark of night fishing the shoreline of a lake in the middle winter; such are the year-round fishing options. The one thing about Rotorua is that it has trout and plenty of them. What's more, they grow very big!

The Rotorua Lakes District has 13 fishable lakes and dozens of rivers within a one-hour drive of the city centre. The region is a great place to explore for anglers and non-anglers alike. Accessing the rivers and lakes is very easy and does not require long walks or four-wheel-drive vehicles. Most of the lakes were formed by volcanic activity long ago. The last major eruption was of Mt Tarawera on 10 June 1886.

While a few of the lakes, like Lake Rotorua, are shallow, and some may only be a few hectares in area, all hold very good numbers of fish. But the key to fishing success on these stillwaters is to understand the fish movements in relation to the season, their eating habits and spawning behaviour.

The main food sources for Rotorua trout is smelt, inanga cockabullies and koura (freshwater crayfish), although they will at times feed prolifically on invertebrates such as snails, beetles and dragonfly nymphs. Although these lakes are not primarily insect-based fisheries, there are times when techniques used need to imitate the food items. Techniques include using large streamer-type flies fished just below the surface in spring when the fish are actively chasing smelt. Dark-coloured Woolly Bugger patterns may be fished slow and deep at night when large trout cruise the edge of the lake in search of cockabullies and koura.

The most popular lakes are Rotorua, Rotoiti, Tarawera, Okataina and Rotoma. Their popularity is mainly due to their history of regularly producing trophy trout; they all have signposted fishing access sites and are well-documented in Fish and Game booklets and maps.

The prime time for fly fishers to target trophy fish is when they move inshore and congregate at river mouths prior to spawning. This pilgrimage usually starts around April/May when the temperature starts cooling, heralding the onset of winter and many of the biggest trout are taken in the hours of darkness. Before hitting the water,

Parsons Glory – a Kiwi classic, Matuku-style fly, developed over a century ago and still a very deadly pattern, especially on Lake Rotorua.

OPPOSITE: Two fish of a lifetime! David Bach has every reason to be delighted with these 7.25 kg and 6 kg (16 lb. and 13 lb.) brown trout taken on the 2005 season opening morning at the Ohau Channel.

There is a lifetime's fishing in the Rotorua District.

take time to visit the local tackle stores; they will have their fingers on the pulse and will point you to the current hot spots. Evening and night-time fishing can be very exhilarating, the first thing you feel is a sharp tug on your line followed by a frantic splashing, you suddenly realise you are actually hooked onto that noise and the line screaming from your reel indicates a very big fish.

Thermal wonderland with world-famous fisheries.

Lakes Rerewhakaaitu, Rotoehu, Tikitapu (Blue Lake) and Okareka are less popular but still hold good populations of fish and all have unique features that make them very pleasurable to fish. For example, it is not unusual to be the only angler on some of these smaller lakes and when strong winds prevent fishing on the more exposed lakes, finding a sheltered bay on the lee shore of a smaller lake can be very productive. All lakes are easily accessible by car and most can be fished from the shoreline by wading, although a small boat or float tube opens up much more water.

The rivers in the Rotorua Lakes District are also fantastic. Several famed streams flow into Lake Rotorua, including the Ngongotaha, Awahou, Waiteti and Hamurana, which can provide spectacular action at their mouths. The streams are spread all around the lake so regardless of the wind direction you can usually find a lee shore. The inflows regularly produce brown trout over 4.5 kg (10 lb.) so use appropriate tackle if you want a fair chance of landing one of these brutes. When the conditions are right the number of fish they produce is astounding. A prime example is is when the shallow Lake Rotorua heats up in summer and shoals of rainbows congregate at the stream mouths because of the cooler water and feast on the smelt that are there for the same reason. When the action is on, a reasonably competent angler can land half a dozen trout.

The other major catchment of the district is formed by the rivers flowing through the Kaingaroa Forest, the largest planted forest in the southern hemisphere. The Rangitaiki River and its tributaries offer literally hundreds of kilometres of fishable water. While many of these rivers are small and clear, the size of some of the trout they produce is phenomenal.

For the visitor, the best way to pinpoint where to fish in the Rotorua district is to make contact with the tackle stores or fishing guides as these people have many years of local experience and operate a friendly and efficient network; they will always give you the best options, and lots of local tips if you take the time to ask.

Getting There

Rotorua is 233 km (145 miles) from Auckland. Driving takes around three hours at a comfortable pace and the route is well signposted with plenty to see. Rotorua also has a busy domestic airport

Two very different colourations on these rainbows from Lake Tarawera; the dark fish is in drab spawning colours. Keep the fresh silver fish to eat and return the spawners.

with daily flights to major centres throughout New Zealand.

Access

There is excellent access to many of the angling sites around the Rotorua Lakes District. Numerous fishing spots are no more than a stroll from where you park the car, although there are plenty of harder to get to locations for more adventurous anglers. The only area that requires an access permit is the Kaingaroa Forest, obtainable from Kaingaroa Timberlands Management Ltd or their agents. The easiest place to obtain a permit is from:

Independent Securities
66 Tarewa Road
Rotorua
Ph: +64-7-347 8880 or +64-7-350 1234
Fax: +64-7-347 8880
Email: margaret.conn@iscl.co.nz

Be aware that Lake Rotokakahi (Green Lake) is privately owned by local Maori and entry or fishing is forbidden.

Lake Tarawera provides awesome views and great rainbow trout fishing for the whole family.

ABOVE: A large tiger trout – a sterile hybrid of a brook-brown cross.

ABOVE RIGHT: A rare albino rainbow trout at the Ngongotaha hatchery.

Angling

The Rotorua Lakes have been stocked with three or four trout species introduced to New Zealand, although the primary attraction are the rainbow and brown trout which grow to enormous sizes. Some lakes have only rainbow trout but Lake Rotoma has 'tiger trout'; Fish and Game have been releasing this brown/brook hybrid into the lake for some years. They are a pretty fish, with distinctive tiger stripes along the body. Only a handful are caught each year but they do provide an elusive challenge for keen anglers.

Lake Tikitapu (Blue Lake) has been stocked with brook trout (*Salvelinus fontinalis*) – actually a member of the Char family – but they are seldom recaptured.

The waters in this region feature both stocked and wild fisheries; to get a better understanding of how the stocking process works, and the exceptional management of one of the top trout fisheries in the world, visit the Fish and Game hatchery at Ngongotaha (see the Resources section).

Season

There is plenty of water to fish throughout the entire year and the prospects of landing a trophy remain very real in any season. Some lakes remain open to anglers all year while others have a closed season or have restrictions. Bag limits also vary across the District. What follows is a general guide but anglers should refer to the Eastern Region Fish and Game Sports Fishing Regulations or ask a local tackle store or the helpful folks at Fish and Game.

Fish and Game regulations are conveniently located throughout the district.

Lakes Okareka, Rerewhakaaitu, Rotoehu, Rotomahana, Rotorua and Tikitapu are open for fly fishing all year with a bag limit of eight trout.

Lake Rotoma is open all year except for specific winter shoreline areas.

Lakes Okataina, Rotoiti and Tarawera are open 1 October – 30 June except for specific areas.

The Ohau Channel connecting Lake Rotorua to Lake Rotoiti is open 1 October – 30 June.

Rivers, streams and other waterways in the region all have specific seasons and regulations which need to be checked before you fish.

The opening of the season for those waters closed over winter is keenly awaited by tens of thousands of anglers and Rotorua is abuzz with anticipation leading up to the first day of October each year. Generations of anglers have religiously flocked to favourite spots for over a hundred years to try their luck on opening morning. One of the great Kiwi traditions is the start of the season at the Ohau Channel. Hundreds of anglers brave the pre-dawn cold to secure their spots while late arrivals patiently queue for their turn. You may have to fish shoulder to shoulder but the atmosphere is always festive and friendly with whole families attending. What's more, the numbers and size of trout landed can be quite phenomenal.

Techniques and Tactics

The lake-fishing techniques that are successful in the Rotorua Lakes District have been refined over decades and once mastered will produce results in many other waters as well. Fishing with one or two large lures (streamer flies) in size 8 or 6 on floating or slow-sinking lines is the favoured technique. With tandem rigs a good lead fly selection is a dull green, brown or black fly such as a Woolly Bugger. Try a smelt-type pattern in grey or silver as a point fly. For night fishing, the tail fly can be switched to a lumo pattern such as a Doll Fly or small Marabou (size 8–10). We find that a figure-of-eight hand-knitting technique creates just the right action to provoke strikes.

Opening morning at the Ohau Channel is an old Kiwi tradition. It may be a little less solitary than normal, but there are always some phenomenal rainbows and browns landed and a great atmosphere of mass anticipation and camaraderie.

Fishing a Booby deep along the bottom. This angler employs a stripping basket to make casting easier.

But when the fish are visibly feeding on smelt, the retrieve can be at a much faster pace. A #8 or #9 rod is a good choice for long distance casts with large streamer flies, especially when the wind is blowing.

Newer techniques that have proved very successful (if a little controversial) include the use of a buoyant Glo Bug, delivered in a heave-and-leave fashion, and the Booby Fly. This method is used to fish a drop-off or weed edge on the lake with a fast sinking line and let the rig settle to the bottom. The line is held taunt so any taps can be detected but the line is not retrieved. The Booby Fly is cast and allowed to settle and then retrieved in little short strips and allowed to settle after each strip. Both these techniques are absolutely lethal and catch fish both in daylight and after dark, but are frowned upon by some fly

anglers who stick to more traditional methods.

Fishing the rivers and streams with weighted nymphs suspended below a small indicator or dry fly will also produce plenty of fish. The use of traditional wet flies and emerger patterns can also be particularly effective at change of light during the warmer months.

An ideal rig for fishing the rivers is a #6 weight outfit with a floating line, which will cover most conditions. A selection of sinking lines is also a good idea for winter; swinging a streamer fly through deeper pools, fast runs and under banks which will pick up fish that can't be covered with a nymph.

Flies and Rigs

The vast majority of lake fishing is done with large streamer flies also known as lures. There are many effective patterns developed in New Zealand and now used throughout the world. Hook sizes tend to be towards the large end of the scale, with anything from sizes 10 to 4 recommended for giant fish on heavy breaking strain leaders. The most common rig is a one- or two-fly set-up. With this tandem rig, the point fly is tied directly to the bend of the lead-fly hook, with around 30 cm (12 in.) of tippet in 3 to 5 kg (6.6 to 11 lb.) breaking strain. For the leader to the rod use 2 to 3 m (6 ft. 6 in. to 9 ft. 9 in.) of straight tippet material in the same breaking strain. During daylight hours, fish a smelt pattern such as a Parson's Glory or a dark Woolly Bugger. At the change of light or after dark, change to a small lumo Doll Fly as a lead fly and a Black Marabou on the point. River-fishing rigs are fairly similar to those used in other North Island locations. A two-nymph rig with a small indicator on a 3 m (9 ft. 9 in.) leader will work in most places. Nymph sizes from 12 to 16 will cover most scenarios. A gold-ribbed Hare's Ear in size 12 or similar, dressed not too heavily, and roughly dubbed is a great generic nymph pattern as is the Pheasant Tail.

Fish surface flies – such as emergers and dries – when surface activity is visible. This usually occurs in the rivers from around October and November onwards and is triggered by warmer weather. Hatches of sedge and caddis start at the change of light and often last until well after dark. At this time of year food sources include caddis and beetles. During the summer months fish will rise throughout the day to grasshoppers, crickets, cicadas and other terrestrials. Use large attractor flies which will imitate most of the types of insects

available. Combined with small unweighted nymphs such as Dutch COC Emerger, they will help you to cover both surface and sub-surface feeders.

Tips and Tricks

Much of the fishing in the Rotorua region is conducted after dark. When night fishing, try charging up lumo flies using a camera flash; but be sure to hide it under your jacket so as not to scare the fish. Any little current entering these lakes will attract fish, so look for areas like creeks, drains and culverts to target fish. Vary the speed of retrieve. Don't wade straight in, as fish cruise the shoreline. When river fishing, make sure your flies are properly weighted so they are getting down to the fish. Play around with leader lengths, fly sizes and flyline sink rates. Use long, drag-free casts with lighter nymphs or short tight casts with plenty of mends when using heavy flies.

FAR LEFT: Smelt imitation patterns are effective year round.

LEFT: Winter nights can produce excellent fishing, but with sub-zero temperatures you need to dress for the occasion.

Flora and Fauna

The sulphurous smell of the Rotorua Lakes District provides an ever-present reminder of an area best known for its geothermal activity. There are a wide variety of terrains in this vast region including the Kaiangaroa Forest, the largest pine forest in the southern hemisphere; a magnificent redwood forest just minutes from the main centre; and vast areas of native bush surrounding dormant volcanic peaks. The high ranges that are the birthplace of many of the rivers are typical of the North Island's bush, with ponga (native fern trees), cabbage trees and vast areas of dense manuka (ti tree) and scrub. Occasional spires of a kauri, rimu or totara trees give the bush its almost prehistoric look.

Introduced mammals like the pig, deer, wallaby and bush-tailed possum are fairly common in this environment; as are the ferrets, stoats and weasels that were introduced to control the booming rabbit population. Unfortunately, they found native birds a far easier source of food and are now classified as pests. The nocturnal kiwi and other native birds share the bush with introduced species like the starling and sparrow. One of the most common birds is the Indian mynah, seen on every roadside casually walking aside as cars speed past. Kahu (harrier hawks) are the birds of prey often spotted as they visit roadsides to feast on road kill and the young of other birds. Popular game birds can also be found in the pastoral and forest regions of the Rotorua district with a variety of ducks, ring neck pheasants and Californian quail. These game birds are managed by the Fish and Game Council and hunting rules and seasons should be checked prior to any sport shooting.

Although New Zealand has no snakes, it does have a few reptiles, and local and introduced frogs and lizards are occasionally spotted close to the rivers. The native frog is silent, while introduced species are easily identified with a call that can be confused with a motorbike in the distance.

Why the trout get so large. A large rainbow reveals its recent feast of monster-sized inanga.

Two happy anglers with a Lake Rotoiti rainbow jack taken in shallow water on the lakeshore.

A fat 8 lb. hen taken on a lumo fly.

A good red stag from the Rotorua region.

A keen hunter uses a mountainbike to access thick bush.

ABOVE: Lake Rotorua, the region's largest lake.
OPPOSITE: Rafting the Kaituna River. One of many adrenalin rushes in Rotorua's adventure playground.

THINGS TO REMEMBER

DO:

- Allow plenty of time for fishing the Rotorua Lakes District as it has a lot of area to explore.
- Consult the local tackle store for up-to-date fishing information.
- Drive with your headlights on in the forests at all times.
- Get a permit if going into the forestry area.
- Let someone know where you are going and when you will return.
- Carry plenty of essentials of warm clothes, food and drink.
- Take a break every hour when fishing lakes at night.

DON'T:

- Go into the forestry or bush areas without maps and a compass.
- Drink the river water without boiling it, it may contain the giardia parasite.
- Touch any possum traps or baits they may be poison.
- Drive off-road unless you have experience.
- Be too keen to wade into the lakes. If other anglers are on the shore, check with them first.
- Shine torches into the lake when night fishing.

THINGS TO DO

Rotorua is full of things to do and see, making it one of New Zealand's premier tourist destinations. The stunning scenery with all kinds of geothermal wonders from bubbling mud to geysers will satisfy all nature lovers. With the possibilities of activities like white-water rafting, four-wheel-drive treks, mountain biking, bush walks and Zorbing, if you're looking for a bit of extra adventure. For those wanting to get an understanding of Maori culture, there are numerous opportunities from enjoying a hangi meal (food cooked traditionally in an underground oven), traditional song and dance, arts and crafts and recreated villages that offer a glimpse of life in the early times.

Maps

Topographical Maps for this region are: 260-U15 (Ngongotaha), 260-U16 (Rotorua), 260-V15 (Edgecumbe), 260-V16 (Tarawera) and 260-V17 (Murupara). They are not required for angling but should be carried if you are looking at tramping or other outdoor activities involving prolonged periods in the bush.

Resources

Hamill's Hunting & Fishing BOP
1271 Fenton Street, Rotorua
Ph: +64-7-348 3147
Fax: +64-7-348 3146
Email: hamrotnz@xtra.co.nz

Eastern Region Fish and Game Council
Ngongotaha Hatchery
Paradise Valley Road, Ngongotaha
Ph: +64-7-357 5501
Fax: +64-7-357 5503

Department of Conservation
Rotorua Lakes Area Office
14–16 Scott Street, Rotorua
Ph: +64-7-348 3610
Fax: +64-7-349 3690
Email: rotorualakesinfo@doc.govt.nz

Treetops Lodge
351 Kearoa Road
RD 1, Horohoro, Rotorua
Ph. +64-7-333 2066
Fax: +64-7-333 2065
Email: info@treetops.co.nz

www.rotoruanz.com
Has an in-depth guide to all of Rotorua's activities, accommodation, and fishing guides.

www.fishandgame.org.nz

Rotorua is well serviced with accommodation, ranging from camp grounds, cabins and backpacker lodgings to motels and hotels or exclusive retreats and lodges.

- Action and Adventure: Gondola (cable car) and luge rides, hunting, fishing, mountain biking, hiking or leisurely bush walks, white-water rafting, kayaking, horse trekking, 4WD, wild fowl shooting, kids fishing days at the Ngongotaha Hatchery.
- Eco and Nature: Geothermal sights, aerial sight seeing, Fairy Springs trout pools and Kiwi Encounter farm visits, wetland bird watching, forest walks.
- Health and Relaxation: Thermal pools, guided and unguided nature walks, lake tours, sight seeing, golf, massage.
- Arts and Gardens: Garden tours, Arts and Crafts markets, traditional Maori carving, museums.
- Food and Wine: Cafés and restaurants.
- Shows and Events: Events happen throughout the year at the Soundshell and there is a regular craft market.

'He told us about Christ's disciples being fisherman, and we were left to assume … that all great fishermen on the Sea of Galilee were fly fishermen and that John, the favourite, was a dry-fly fisherman.'

Norman Maclean, *A River Runs Through It*

MANGATUTU STREAM

3

MA(STREAM); NGATUTU (SWAMP REEDS) – STREAM OF THE REEDS.

The scenic backdrop to the Mangatutu Stream is one of those classic New Zealand vistas that typify tourism promotion material – rolling hills, lush green meadows and cows grazing lazily beneath rows of poplar trees swaying gently in the breeze. By contrast, the upper stream flows through ancient dense native forest with dappled light seeping through the shade of the giant canopy. Throw in a mosaic of droplets dancing above the pure sparkling water of a stony stream and an abundant trout population of good-sized wild rainbows and browns, flat easy access and clear banks for fly casting and you have an angler's paradise.

The Mangatutu Stream is a significant tributary of the Puniu River and runs for 40 km (25 miles) from its source in the Pureora Forest to the confluence with the Puniu. The upper half runs through indigenous forest while the more popular lower sections meander through pastoral farmland. Here the stream winds in large oxbows through the soft clay soils, allowing anglers to take short cuts between stretches in search of new water or to give other anglers plenty of room.

This water is highly prized among local anglers and receives considerable angler interest, especially early in the season. Drift-dive surveys confirm that compared to other North Island rivers, the Mangatutu holds high numbers of adult rainbows and browns. A few guides bring clients into this area but both the Puniu and Waipa catchments have several superb streams and rivers to choose from so the Mangatutu is not overly pressured. You could fish for many weeks within an hour's drive of the Mangatutu without covering the hundreds of kilometres of trout habitat in the Waipa River system.

Other recommended fly-fishing destinations in the vicinity include the Waipa River, Kaniwhaniwha stream, Ngakoaohia Stream, Moakurarua Stream, and Puniu River.

Getting There

Located within half an hour's drive of Hamilton and two hours' of Auckland, this region in general offers excellent options for day-tripping anglers. The Mangatutu is one of the most accessible and productive fisheries within reasonable driving distance of Auckland and Hamilton International Airports, making it a good choice for those visitors with little time.

You can drive to the stream by heading south of Hamilton on State Highway 3 via Te Awamutu and Kihikihi and turning left onto Wharepuhunga Road. A 10-minute drive will bring you to Lethbridge Road. Continue southbound on Wharepuhunga Road past Lethbridge Road a short distance to Wharepuhunga Bridge.

Parachute Adams – a derivative of a very old American pattern. It is extremely versatile and effective as a mayfly imitation; will often tempt trout even when there is no rise on.

OPPOSITE: Prospecting in the riffles at the head of a pool.

Access

The most fishable water is in the middle reaches between Lethbridge Road upstream to the Wharepuhunga Bridge. There are also some excellent spots downstream of Lethbridge Road but this lower section is more challenging with fencing, blackberry and corridors of willows all creating obstacles. The streambed in these lower reaches becomes congested with willows and log falls but there is still plenty of fishable water for those prepared to walk and explore.

In the upper reaches above Wharepuhunga Road bridge, the stream is very diminutive and shallow but still holds good numbers of large fish in the numerous deep holes, under banks and in the heads of rapids. On one occasion I nearly stood on a large brown concealed beneath the overhung grass bank, while trying to stalk a rainbow a few metres across on the other bank. Although it requires skill and imagination, this water will certainly appeal to those looking to stalk large trout in a small waterway. There is a public access reserve along both banks extending upstream of the Wharepuhunga Bridge into the forest, but you need to look around to find

Prime water in the upper reaches above Wharepuhunga Bridge.

access to the stream and reasonable casting opportunities.

There is no public accessway below Wharepuhunga Bridge but, as with most of New Zealand, the landowners are usually very happy to grant permission providing you ask first.

Angling

This small stream is very clear, flowing over a stable rock and pebble bed in an attractive sequence of well-defined pools and runs. There are fish up to 2.5 kg (5 lb.) but the average is around 1.5 kg (3.3 lb.). The majority of rainbows spend their entire lives in the Mangatutu and its tributaries, spawning throughout the stream and feeders during autumn and winter. In contrast, the browns are not resident year round and undertake a seasonal migration into the Waikato River, New Zealand's longest, which arises on the slopes of Mt Ruapehu in the Tongariro National Park and runs from Lake Taupo north-west into the Tasman Sea. These browns return to the Mangatutu in spring as the waters of the Waikato become too warm.

All the waterways in the Waikato region become swollen and discoloured with heavy rainfall but also clear quickly. Check the weather forecast or call a local tackle store or guide to check on stream conditions. After prolonged, or torrential rain, the waterways in this region

The scenic middle reaches looking downstream towards Lethbridge Road.

will be unfishable, so check the weather to avoid disappointment.

Besides the idyllic rural scenery, one of the most alluring aspects of the Mangatutu is the opportunity to land large trout of both species from a petite waterway. The middle reaches are perfect for beginners or for light-tackle enthusiasts looking for an exhilarating workout on a #3 to #5 weight rod, with only short accurate casts required to cover most fish. Our last visit to the Mangatutu was on a blistering hot summer's day and we fished the 10 km (6.2 mile) stretch above Lethbridge Road, landing five rainbows, with the biggest being about 2 kg (4.4 lb.) and dropping a large brown estimated at over 2.5 kg (5 lb.). We are by no means the most proficient of anglers, so this result displays the quality of angling available to the average fly fisher.

This stream is ideally suited for both nymphing and dry-fly fishing although a sinking line and small wet fly could be put to good effect fished downstream under banks and overhanging willows. These small clear waters require a good degree of finesse in your stalking technique, especially if you are targeting larger fish or the ever-wary browns. Keep your clothing colours drab; cross the stream below reaches you are about to fish; be aware of your shadow and stay low and off the skyline on the higher banks. There is an abundance of fish through most sections, so move slowly and scan all visible sections carefully. Prime holding zones for fish include areas of bottom (not visible even with quality Polaroids)

such as the deeper pools, white water, channels beneath banks and areas obscured by vegetation. Larger fish and browns in particular avoid sunlight during the day, so fish every shaded spot to which you can get a fly. A nymph or dry fly dropped underneath – or hard against – the many overhanging willows is deadly on a bright day, although you may lose the odd fly to the trees.

Don't lose faith if you hook several tiddlers as the next fish from the same water could easily be a fat angry adult that drags you off down the rapids. There's not much room in some of the pools and reaches, and hooked fish will make every attempt to rush either up or downstream. This means a hot pursuit and some nimble footwork if you aim to stay connected.

Dry-fly action can be phenomenal even if there is no obvious feeding activity. Mangatutu fish are ambush specialists and will dart out of cover to grab a well-presented dry without hesitation. The last fish I landed on the lower Mangatutu grabbed my Parachute Adams as it landed in a feeding lane in a tight pocket between two willows. After leaping into the

Fish the deep shaded runs under the willows.

Keep well back from the banks when searching for fish.

ABOVE: This hungry rainbow tried to swallow a Parachute Adams dry in one gulp.

ABOVE RIGHT: A hard-fighting speckled rainbow makes a desperate break for the bottom.

overhanging branches and crashing around the pool, I finally managed to subdue a beautiful 1.5 kg (3.3 lb.) rainbow jack with the fly lodged securely in the back of his tongue. These are the magic takes that you dream about, but they can happen in a flash so you need to stay alert and be accurate with your casts. Upon release, the jack I caught swam casually over to his territory and returned to station; no doubt he is waiting for the next artificial fly to drift his way.

The terrain is very easy going and this is a great destination for those who struggle with their mobility, or for non-fishing companions to tag along for a picnic and a refreshing dip in one of the many pools. There may well be other anglers on the stream, especially on weekends, but with so much easily fishable water you should have little trouble finding an unfished section. Always make the effort to have a quick chat with other anglers as most are eager to swap and share information and will usually provide some local knowledge to get you started.

Season

Open from 1 October to 30 June. The water above Lethbridge Road bridge is reserved for fly fishing only and the bag limit is five trout with a minimum size of 30 cm (12 in.).

Techniques and Tactics

If you have a companion, a great approach is to take a bank each and spot for each other. The elevated clay banks on the outside of bends are perfect for spotting fish, but often the best strategy is for the angler on the opposite bank to cover fish under your bank while you direct proceedings. This just leaves the fish in the middle to squabble over.

The stream is very easy to cross and can be fished easily in shorts and sneakers in the warmer months and thigh waders are perfect to keep dry in cooler months.

It is not uncommon to spot several fish holding close together. Try carefully covering the downstream fish first, taking care to keep false casts and the fly line out of the trout's window of vision. If you're skilled and lucky, you can hook and lead the first fish downstream and return to target the next in line.

Normally, you won't get too many second chances when fishing to brown trout. Make your first cast count and keep your fly selection small

It doesn't come any easier than this for access and casting.

and natural. Once a fish has refused a fly they can be very difficult to tempt and usually depart or simply remain on the bottom. The rainbows tend to be far more accommodating and will revisit your flies several times before taking. If there are trout rising or feeding anywhere between midwater and the surface, tie on two different dry flies. You could even try giving the line a small twitch if the fish are not showing interest in dead drifted flies.

Small-stream angling doesn't require long-distance casting but having a good repertoire of alternative casts and good accuracy will improve your chances of reaching fish in difficult lies without disturbing them. Backhand casts, roll casts, steeple casts and even bow-and-arrow casts can be very useful where impediments like vegetation and banks negate the use of a more orthodox cast. Keep the fly line off the water by false casting and try to land the fly line, leader and fly as lightly as possible in a parachute-type fashion. This can be achieved by slowing your rod speed on the last forward cast and releasing the cast at a slightly higher angle, allowing the line to balloon gently onto the surface.

Long leaders and positioning yourself correctly relative to the target is important. It's easy to stalk in too close to a fish before you spot it, but providing you haven't disturbed the fish you can carefully backtrack or creep carefully into cover or even lie down and crawl away to a safe casting distance.

Either spotting with caution or about to take a nap.

In a normal downstream flow, one of the best spots to present drag-free flies with the least possibility of detection is from directly downstream of the fish; where the angler and fly line remain in the blind spot of fish naturally facing upstream into the current. Depending on the turbulence of the current, this may allow a drag-free drift directly over the fish without the need for any mending.

Another good habit to adopt is ensuring the fly line and rig have drifted well below your target before gently lifting the line off for the next cast. Many fish are disturbed simply by over-anxious anglers commencing the next cast while the line or flies are still in the trout's window of vision. Just like a good billiards or golf player, the fly angler should plan the best approach to present the flies close to the target in a natural drag-free drift. One of the biggest obstacles is current, which can create any number of problems with drag on the flies and fly line. The versatile fisher can overcome many of these obstacles by picking the best angle of approach and with correct mending of the fly line to neutralise the distortions of current. As

an example, you will often find fish sitting hard under a riffle or rapid at the head of a pool or facing downstream in a side eddy. Try positioning yourself upstream, casting downstream and landing the flies well above your quarry and immediately flicking slack loops of line from your rod tip onto the water to create a resistance-free drift downstream over the fish. This is a better approach than the standard upstream cast as it allows more time to sink the flies.

Flies and Rigs

Given the delicate nature of small streams and high visibility issues associated with clear water, you will find strike rates improve markedly by using long tapered leaders with a 2.5 to 3 kg (5 to 6.6 lb.) tippet. Tapered leaders roll out cleanly and enable a proficient caster to land flies delicately with minimum surface disturbance. Use a 4–5 m (13–16 ft.) leader for dry-fly fishing. Adapt the same leader for nymph fishing by attaching a small tuft of yarn or natural sheep's wool with a removable indicator knot at the appropriate length along the leader.

Parachute Adams (foreground) and a traditional Adams. Two dry flies we would never be without.

A dry fly and dropper combination is a good starting option, suspending a lightly weighted or unweighted nymph up to 1 m (39 in.) behind a dry fly. With this rig you can cover both the surface and the streambed. Use a small or medium-sized dry-fly pattern that is buoyant and easy to spot, and which acts as an indicator for any takes on the nymph.

Remember to strike immediately if a fish takes the nymph, but hesitate and allow time for the fish to turn before lifting the rod on a dry-fly take. There has been many a time when we have failed to hook good fish by making over-zealous strikes.

Our favourite dry flies for the Mangatutu include the Grey Wulff, Parachute Adams (an Adams with a tuft of white yarn to improve buoyancy and aid visibility), Goddard Caddis, Twilight Beauty, Black Gnat and Hardy's Favourite. Effective nymphs are Caddis Larvae in green or brown, Pheasant Tails, Willow Grubs and little Black Stoneflies. If you're lucky you may strike fish feeding on cicada or beetles; switch to a large terrestrial dry fly – then hang on for some vicious surface action. The cooler months are more suited to covering midwater and the bottom with a pair of bead-head nymphs tied in natural patterns – like Hare's Ear nymphs – are a solid choice for this technique, but be prepared to offer a variety of sizes and weights.

Tips and Tricks

If you have a companion, rig one outfit with a dry or dry and dropper, and the other with two nymphs. This way you can cover more layers of water with the two different approaches and simply switch rods if you want to try something different. This certainly saves valuable fishing time otherwise wasted by switching rigs. If one of the techniques is significantly more successful, switch both rods to that technique. As a general rule, on any water it makes good common sense to adopt different tactics when fishing with others. Start your fishing expeditions with different techniques, rigs and flies and slowly refine your

strategy based on the combined success or lack thereof of the group. If you are not striking fish, change something – your flies, leader, fly line or move to another piece of water. There is no merit in thrashing the same beat if you're not catching fish, especially on a small stream. Another good option is to have some lunch, enjoy the scenery or take a nap.

Generally, small sparsely dressed natural imitations will catch a larger proportion of adult fish and are more effective in most situations for deceiving brown trout in the Mangatutu. However, the dominant fish in a reach will often be hard on the bottom in the deeper pools or channels and the angler is faced with sinking one or two small nymphs quickly to reach the strike zone. Rather than increase the fly size and weight, it is worth investing in some tungsten putty, which can be moulded onto the leader above the flies. This is a great weapon to have in your fly vest when trying to present small nymphs at depth or in fast-flowing water.

Equipment and Apparel

Shorts, a long-sleeved shirt for sun protection and a pair of sports shoes with good grip on the soles is all you need in warmer months. The most critical item of apparel is a quality pair of Polaroids, and remember a good hat, sunscreen and insect repellent.

The basic ingredients for a day's hunting on the Mangatutu.

The only redeeming feature of the angler's curse – delicious ripe blackberries.

Flora and Fauna

Waipa District has a temperate climate with plentiful water and very fertile soils, making the area well suited to agriculture and horticulture. The district boasts a number of impressive natural features, such as indigenous forests, peat lakes and swamps and hydro lakes providing significant wildlife habitats, especially for wetland birds. The Waikato and Waipa Rivers are also significant environmental features and the scenic quality of the Waipa has meant that large tracts of its landscape are now recognised as special landscape character areas. This region is one of New Zealand's largest inland ecological islands with ongoing efforts to eradicate mammalian pests and noxious exotic plants from Maungatautari's indigenous forest and the restoration of the mountain's native ecology.

THINGS TO REMEMBER

DO:

- Take care with the clay banks as erosion is a problem in the Mangatutu watershed. Anglers should keep back from the edges to prevent further damage created through water flow and livestock.
- Release fish if they are not healthy fat specimens. If possible, leave the fish in the water and unhook it without touching it. Support fish gently upright in the current until they regain enough energy to swim away with vigour.
- Check with the landowner before parking on private property.
- Take a chilly bin (insulated cooling bin) or cool bag if you are keeping fish to eat, especially in the summer.

DON'T:

- Leave valuables in your car.
- Climb on farmers' fence wires. Always cross at a strainer post, use a gate or slide underneath. This prevents damage to the farmer's property and yourself (many wire fences are electrified or are barbed wire – which damages clothes, waders and flesh).
- Disturb livestock or damage riverbanks or crops.

The correct place to cross farm fences to avoid damage to fencing and waders!

THINGS TO DO

The Waikato is a region of lush green hills, bush and farmland, with exceptional surf on the west coast and many excellent golf courses. Throughout the region you can discover bush-clad mountains, stunning waterfalls, hot mineral pools, beaches and the magnificent limestone glow-worm cavesof Waitomo situated 17 km (10.5 miles) south of Otorohanga on State Highway 37 (off State Highway 3). The Waitomo caves provide a magical experience and black-water rafting, caving and abseiling are unique adventures.

- Eco and Nature: Farm visits, wetland bird watching, farm and forest walks, Otorohanga Kiwi House.
- Health and Relaxation: Golf, massage, thermal pools, nature walks.
- Arts and Gardens: Garden tours, arts and crafts markets, galleries, museums.
- Food and Wine: Cafés, restaurants and wineries.
- Shows and Events: Farmers' markets, film festivals, rock concerts, surfing and wakeboarding competitions, rugby, cricket, rowing regattas, sailing, water-skiing championships, shearing, equestrian shows and wood carving, Balloons over Waikato, Mystery Creek annual agricultural field-days.

Maps

The Mangatutu and other rivers in the vicinity are easy to find on any detailed New Zealand Road Atlas and there is no benefit in acquiring topographical maps. A quality road map booklet such as the AA (Automobile Association) road books are a highly recommended companion for any independent traveller visiting the country. They contain useful information on everything from campgrounds to historic sites.

Resources

www.tourism.net.nz
www.waikatonz.com
www.hamiltoninfo.co.nz
www.waitomocaves.co.nz

Te Awamutu i-Site Visitor Information Centre
1 Gorst Avenue
Phone: +64-7-871 3259
Fax: +64-7-871 2888
Email: ta.info@xtra.co.nz

Hamilton i-Site Visitor Information Centre
Transport Centre
Cnr Bryce & Anglesea Streets
Phone: +64-7-839 3580
Fax: +64-7-839 3127

ABOVE: World-class rock climbing action at Wharepapa South.
RIGHT: Underground playground at Waitomo.

- Action and Adventure: There is no shortage of activities above ground with world-class rock climbing a short drive from the Mangatutu River at Wharepapa South, horse trekking, four-wheel-drive biking, hot-air ballooning, paragliding, gliding, skydiving, surfing, sea fishing, jet boating, rafting and kayaking, mountain biking, clay target and wild duck shooting.

'Many men go fishing their entire lives without knowing it is not fish they are after.'

Henry David Thoreau

WHIRINAKI RIVER
WHIRINAKI — TO LEAN, OR THE BUTTRESS OF A HOUSE

f you have ever dreamt of a fairytale stream dancing clear and cool through primeval forests and meadows of wild flowers, the Whirinaki River is the place for you. This is a water to be treasured, not for the numbers or size of trout, but for the sheer magnificence and purity of the experience.

Rising deep in the ancient Whirinaki rainforest, the river winds northwards through the tribal lands of the Ngati Whare, past Minginui village and Te Whaiti, finally joining the world-renowned Rangitaiki River near Murupara.

Maori have lived here probably as long as the oldest trees still standing and continue with their traditional responsibilities as guardians of the forest. This was one of New Zealand's most famous conservation battlegrounds, where people fought to save a magnificent native forest. Today Whirinaki is protected as a forest park and everyone can enjoy its beauty through a comprehensive network of walks, tracks and huts.

Of all the outstanding waters in this region, the Whirinaki ranks at the top of our list for its unsurpassed natural beauty and other qualities that make it a world-class fly-fishing experience. Angling companions who introduced us to the Whirinaki had promised quality fishing but we were quite unprepared for the area's incredible scenery.

There is a wide variety of water to whet anyone's appetite. The headwaters are tightly guarded by bush and slowly expand through the upper reaches on a winding path through the mature native forest of the Forest Park. Downstream the river enters a gorge section with slow glides interspersed with picturesque pools, becoming gradually swifter and more boisterous in the willow-lined section. The lower section is predominantly big, slow pools where the

watercourse has carved deep into the hillsides to create impressive overhanging cliffs. Near the end of its journey, the river flows through farmland and corridors of trees before spilling into the Rangitaiki River. There are many kilometres of first-class water to explore and it would take weeks to get to know all of it intimately.

Getting There

The nearest domestic airport with regular daily flights from other main centres is Rotorua. The upper river in the Whirinaki Forest Park is approximately an 80 km drive south-east of Rotorua along State Highway 38. The Whirinaki Forest Park lies between the wilderness of Te Urewera National Park and the endless ranks of exotic pine trees in the massive Kaingaroa Forest.

Most visitors come via this route, although you can also drive from the coastal township of Whakatane in the Bay of Plenty up the Rangitaiki Valley. From central Auckland it takes approximately 4.5 hours to reach Minginui village via Rotorua.

Pheasant Tail – always carry a selection of these nymphs. Particularly effective in clear water as a natural nymph imitation. Small sizes will take big fish!

OPPOSITE Anglers' paradise – Whirinaki River above Minginui.

Wrestling a strong fish out of the current

Make sure you have all your necessary supplies, including fishing tackle, before heading into this isolated region. There are several excellent sports stores in Rotorua with a full range of fly-fishing equipment. When we fish the upper river we usually fill up with petrol and get camping supplies at Murupara before heading on to Minginui. The highway ends at Te Whaiti where you turn off onto the sealed road to Minginui. If you miss the Minginui turn-off you hit the gravel access road 27, which winds through the Te Urewera National Park to Lake Waikaremoana.

Access

To fish in the upper sections take the River Road out the back of Minginui. There are several marked access points and obvious tracks to rest areas and the river. Drive slowly and carefully on this rough gravel section, as the road narrows and, despite being in a remote area, it is used frequently by tourists, trampers, hunters, forestry and DOC workers and possum trackers. As with other back roads in New Zealand, some users are inclined to speed, so stay alert.

There is great water downstream of Minginui and there are a few tracks providing access through the scrub, but much of this section runs through private farmland. You need to visit the farmers or get permission before venturing across their paddocks. This also applies to much of the middle and lower-river stretches west of Te Whaiti, which can be reached from Troutbeck and Whirinaki Roads. There is also a logging road just downstream of Te Whaiti, off State Highway 38.

In good weather most of the river can be reached in a conventional 2WD but, as with many New Zealand locations, a four-wheel drive is handy, especially after heavy rain.

Angling

The Whirinaki is blessed with a healthy population of rainbow and brown trout that average around 1.5kg (3.3 lb.) but they tend to congregate in certain sections of river at different times of the year and during varying river flows. During autumn and early winter before the season closes, you can often stumble across pockets of water full of rainbows running upstream to spawn, while other areas remain comparatively barren. Even within runs and pools you will find fish concentrated in selective pockets at different times of the day.

It pays to take a mobile approach to a day's fishing. We often drive into a location and tramp into a chosen area, and quickly cover a kilometre or so of water to get a feel for trout numbers — 'fishability factor', as we like to call it. If we don't encounter good numbers of fish or they have their mouths shut, we head back to the car to try elsewhere. On one particular day, a group of us headed off to fish the upper river in an idyllic area of shady native bush interspersed with grassy glades and shingle river flats. Unfortunately, despite walking a fair distance, we encountered only a few solitary fish sulking in the depths of deep pools and these specimens flatly refused to look at the nymphs we offered. After a few hours we headed back to the car and decided to explore below Minginui. Once again, where visibility was good there were no signs of fish but much of the water here is broken and turbulent as it rushes through a series of rapids and reaches. The four in our group split into pairs and started prospecting the edges and heads of some likely-looking pools with tandem rigs of small natural nymph patterns. Plenty of good casts to likely pockets of water failed to elicit a single take, so two of us decided to add small fluffy indicators

to our leaders and switch our approach to concentrate on flicking short blind casts into likely lies in the rapids, broken water and shallow riffles. Within a few casts we were both catching small but hard-fighting rainbows and as soon as we shared our newfound tactic with our companions they were quickly hooked up to chubby, feisty rainbows.

These are not the easiest of waters to fish but once you know more about them your strike

LEFT: Local fly-fishing guru Dean Macmillan taking his trusty motorbike into the forest.

BELOW: A beautiful fat Whirinaki brown.

Warren and Kent watching a cruising fish.

lost several good browns to sunken obstacles and now mainly use 4 kg (8.8 lb.) monofilament with superior abrasion resistance. Go hard on your fish from hook up, there are some large trout in this medium-sized river and they will have no hesitation in bolting downstream through rapids and pools. If this happens, be prepared for the chase because if you don't run after your fish it will normally get the better of you, but watch those slippery rocks!

rate will improve rapidly. The important lessons are to cover plenty of water and not to waste too much time on the tempting depths of the beautiful pools. During daylight the Whirinaki fish feed in the broken water so focus your attention on the riffles and turbulent sections with either nymph or dry fly. Hooking a fish is of course only half the battle in these waters, as the wily inhabitants are experts at using the fast water, boulders, sunken logs and willows to break free. Keep to a minimum of 3 kg (6.6 lb.) monofilament to maximise your chances of landing fish and use plenty of drag on the reel and sideways pressure on the rod to lead fish away from snags. We have

On warm calm evenings in the summer months there can be some impressive evening hatches. As the sun drops, fish will start moving around and take station in the heads and tails of pools. Try skating a sedge or caddis imitation with an emerger pattern 30 cm (12 in.) behind, or swing a team of tiny wet flies across the tail of pools. Don't be surprised if you start catching a lot of small fish, which can be very greedy and a bit of a pest. Perseverance will often pay dividends. Again, move around and cover as many rising fish as possible. If there isn't much surface activity, try fishing a medium-sinking line downstream and slowly retrieve a Red Setter or Hamill's Killer close to the bottom. There are trophy-sized fish in this beautiful river so don't be fooled by the tiddlers (small fish).

Explore the turbulent pocket water and tail of pools.

You need to be reasonably fit and have a good pair of hiking boots to fish the upper reaches. It is a good hike from the end of River Road and there are many kilometres of beautiful water to explore under the towering canopy of native rainforest. This is a good area to camp overnight to allow more time to explore. Layers of pumice from massive volcanic eruptions hundreds of thousands of years ago in the Okataina area and at Taupo mean that tributary streams and the Whirinaki river are filtered clean and the flow is sparkling clear in the upper reaches. These are delicate small waters with large wary trout that require a careful approach and short, accurate casts. Lighter rod weights between #4 and #6 are recommended, combined with low-visibility floating lines.

Overhanging vegetation provides structure, food and shelter.

Season

Open from 1 October to 30 June. The bag limit is two fish but catch and release is recommended in the upper forest sections.

Techniques and Tactics

All methods of fly fishing will catch fish on the Whirinaki River. The most popular approach is upstream nymph fishing with a single or tandem rig. While this is a good choice for targeting fish higher up the river during daylight in the faster-flowing pockets, current lines and runs; it is not the most productive approach in all water at all times. Keep in mind that much of the riverbed is barren and trout will be spread in patches, often separated by long stretches of empty water. Although rainbows and browns share the river, they tend to occupy different habitats, with browns frequently choosing slower-flowing water. Move carefully upstream and remember to search under banks, around sunken snags, overhanging vegetation and in the back eddies. Brown trout will often hold tight in shallow water and the larger fish are quite nocturnal and easier to target at change of light and after sunset when they start moving and feeding.

If you restrict yourself to fishing a floating line and weighted nymphs to sighted trout you will not be covering all the options. Try to read the water and think like a fish: imagine where a rainbow might be sitting behind a boulder in the rapids or off the edge of a shelf at the head of a deep pool. Likewise, the shady dead water behind an overhanging willow is the perfect place to prospect for a large brown with a dry fly and Willow Grub.

Keen observation and a scientific approach to this river will certainly reward anglers. If you are not raising fish, do something different: search for new habitat, alter your terminal rig, switch to a sinking line and keep analysing your surroundings. Trout are masters of conserving

Ancient forest giants.

energy; they are opportunist hunters who select their feeding and resting lies carefully. They do not operate randomly but are creatures of habit. Once you start to analyse your experiences, you will gain invaluable knowledge on how to locate and tempt trout in any river, lake or stream. Interestingly, in areas where there is moderate to high angling pressure, livestock such as cows, sheep and even dogs swimming do not seem to disturb fish as readily as fishers do. Nor should you be put off by rafts, kayaks or even jet boats as fish seem to accustom to these floating objects relatively easily and will quickly return to feeding. I have hooked fish in the wake of a jet boat heading up rapids, with dogs swimming in the middle of a pool and cattle crossing.

Keep in mind the importance of *structure, food, water conditions, visibility* and *season*.

Structure

Trout like cover, not just to ambush their prey but to avoid predators like shags, eels, larger trout and anglers. In low light, discoloured water and at night they become less wary and will abandon structure for more open feeding stations.

Food

All animals need it but trout are particularly efficient, they will usually select the most nutritious and freely available source of nourishment. They will certainly feed more keenly at certain times depending on the availability of food and how hungry they are. During summer months fish can be very sluggish and difficult to hook during the day once they have tapped into the easy feasts available during the evening hatches. It is still possible to entice a fish but fly selection and presentation becomes critical for success. Trout in this dormant state will not waste much energy to secure a mouthful and the fly needs to be a tempting morsel presented very close to the fish – within half a metre (20 in.).

Water conditions

Regardless of whether you kayak, raft or river fish, a good understanding of water dynamics is always a major advantage. Water at different depths, gradients and across different surfaces will be moving at different speeds and in different directions. If you study a section of river water carefully, you will see a huge variety of fluvial characteristics in various sections of the river. Water can be slow-moving or neutral, flowing upstream in eddies, pressure waves, current lines, whirlpools and bubble lines. Trout love neutral water close to fast-flowing current lines, which act as a fast-food delivery service or sushi train. They can expend very little effort and pop into the current to grab a meal.

Visibility

The old adage applies: if you can see them they can probably see you. Trout instinctively keep a low profile and so should you. Always keep back from the edges, minimise sound and keep your shadow off the water. With the exception of spawning season, you generally do not see larger fish sitting in clear view. Always carefully explore any water where visibility is restricted whether by depth, shade, undercut banks, colouration or broken water.

In conditions where rainfall raises and discolours the water, daytime fishing can be spectacular as fish become less wary in the murky water and intensely focused on devouring the flood of food. Early morning, late evening and night-time are also times when fish that have rested during daylight hours will suddenly switch on. Larger, dominant fish will range over wide areas and anglers need to free themselves from their natural dependence on eyesight and instead rely on their senses of sound and feel. Try a large dark streamer fly swung slowly through the tail of a pool on a sinking line or retrieved up the current in the dark. This is very relaxing fishing and the strikes are electrifying. It is one of the best recipes for targeting seriously big browns; however, don't use a leader under 4.5 kg (10 lb.).

Season

As temperatures begin to cool and autumn takes hold, rainbows start moving upstream and entering the Whirinaki from the Rangitaiki River. Their instincts shift from food to sex and so does their behaviour. At this time large shoals of fish will occupy water that is barren in other seasons. Jacks start aggressively battling for supremacy and can be seen chasing and attacking each other. With each fresh rainfall more fish have the impulse to move further upstream. Some spawn in the lower and middle reaches, but large numbers will make their way progressively up into the thin, shallow forest sections to fulfil their urge to procreate. Before the season closes at the end of June, visiting anglers can have superb fishing for these spawning fish. Flashy and gaudy-coloured nymphs like Glo Bugs or a bright wet-fly pattern such as a pink or orange Zonker with plenty of flashabou tied in are a good choice to fire the aggressive instincts of these trout. The name of the game is to annoy the fish by bouncing flies into their lies to induce a strike.

Flies and Rigs

Approach each section of water with an open mind and before casting merrily away, take some time to analyse the water and anticipate where fish may be holding. As a general rule, floating-line methods such as nymphing and dry fly are best suited to the upper and middle reaches while wet flies on a sinking line can be deadly in

Pondering a fly selection.

Use small natural nymphs. The bead-head provides some weight and sparkle.

the middle and lower Whirinaki. No matter which technique you select, the flies must be presented delicately and naturally so you need to use leader lengths and fly weights that will enable you to get the flies to where the fish are. During winter months a 3 to 4 m (9 ft. 9 in. to 13 ft.) leader should suffice for nymphing, but in the summer a long tapered leader of 4 to 5 m (13 to 16 ft.) is more effective for presenting dry flies, emergers and light nymphs. If you then decide to change to nymphing alone, you can simply attach an indicator at the required length on the leader. (An indicator knot is a handy way of temporarily attaching yarn.)

There are good numbers of browns as well as rainbows in the Whirinaki so keep to smaller sizes, 16 to 12 in natural patterns. Useful nymph patterns include Willow Grubs, Pheasant Tails, Prince Nymphs and Stonefly creepers. Carry several dry-fly patterns including terrestrial imitations like cicadas and Coch-y-Bondhu if the fish are on beetles. Other good all-round dry flies are Black Gnat, Royal Coachman and Soldier Palmer. Don't be afraid to try an emerger pattern or attractor wet fly like a Silver Zulu, March Brown or Winged Hare's Ear on either a floating or sinking line. These can be dynamite when swung across reaches and pools, especially late in the day. Effective large wet flies for use with a sinking line are Black Rabbits and Hamill's Killer. Both these flies can be fished with confidence into darkness and have produced some excellent fish for us when night fishing on North Island rivers.

Tips and Tricks

Whenever we visit the Whirinaki the fish seem to be in a different location and playing by a new set of rules. Despite the potential frustrations for newcomers, the odds of success greatly improve if you are receptive to adaptation and vary your approaches to unlock the best recipe for your chosen water on the day.

There is no definitive answer, but if you start with a few proven strategies it will get you in the hunt quicker. Remember not to spend too much time on pools and think about different ways of getting a fly to a likely spot. If you don't have a medium-sinking line you can adapt your floating line into a sink tip by adding a section of sinking line to the end loop. This is a good use for small sections of old sinking lines and we always carry a selection of sink rates in our fly vests. I like to fish two smaller weighted nymphs in a dropper-style rig rather than attaching a small nymph on a short length of line off the bend of a larger, heavier-weighted nymph. This system allows nymphs to hang independently and reduces the need to use a heavier bomb, which can be difficult to cast on lighter rods and has been responsible for shattering one of my favourite #6 weights. This system also reduces hanging up in the riffles and fast water.

Ensure you have a range of nymphs in various weights to cover water of different depths and speed. A large terrestrial fly with a weighted nymph anywhere from 20 cm to 1 m (8 to 39 in.) below is a great rig for working riffles, rapids and current lines. Dress the dry fly regularly to keep it floating high and use it as a visual indicator of strikes on the suspended nymph.

Equipment and Apparel

The weather in this region is very unpredictable and visitors should be prepared for wind, cold and wet spells even at the height of summer. Frosts occur almost all of the year and the river valley can be fog bound and extremely cold during autumn and winter. High rainfall causes all the rivers in the area to rise very quickly and to discolour but they tend to fall and clear almost as quickly. While anglers should be aware and prepared for rain, certainly do not be put off by higher water levels and discoloured water. We have had some of our best fishing in high water, particularly when fish are running in numbers to the upper-river spawning grounds.

This is often the case with many New Zealand rivers, and the period just after peak flow as the water begins to recede is a prime time to be on the banks with rod in hand. Warm clothing, rainproof gear and boots are recommended. In normal flow the river can be crossed easily, and breathable waders or thigh waders are great for winter expeditions. You can wear a layer of polypropylene, silk, wool or fleece underneath for extra warmth and always wear a quality pair of woollen socks. During warmer months I prefer to fish light in boots and shorts, which are more comfortable for long strolls in the heat of the day. Try some neoprene gaiters. I find them fantastic when spending a lot of time in the riverbeds and bush as they keep shingle, pebbles and annoying debris from dropping into your boots.

Flora and Fauna

The Whirinaki rainforest and Te Urewera National Park together contain the largest area of native forest in the North Island. The Whirinaki Forest Park is administered and cared for by DOC and is open for all to enjoy. You can get up-to-date brochures, information and maps from their centres at Murupara and Waikaremoana or from one of their national offices before you enter the park.

The park comprises elements of volcanic and non-volcanic landforms and soils and the plant and animal life reflect these differences. Whirinaki's most striking feature is its unique podocarp forest. The forest is dominated by towering examples of kahikatea, totara, matai, rimu, miro, beech and tawa.

There are also scrubland flats and grass clearings, wetlands and subalpine vegetation on

the high ridges and peaks.

The park has been described as one of the most primeval forests in the world, with many of the tree species originating from the Jurassic period, 200 million years ago. The BBC filmed the documentary *Walking With Dinosaurs* here.

Birdlife is abundant and diverse. The dense podocarps support high numbers of rare forest birds, especially the North Island kaka, red and yellow-crowned parakeets (kakariki) and New

A good selection of dull-coloured practical clothing for summer expeditions.

Zealand pigeons (kereru). Other notable birds include the blue duck (whio) and the endangered New Zealand falcon.

Besides trout, there are long-finned eels in this river system, along with several other species of native fish. New Zealand's only native mammals, the long-tailed and short-tailed bat, are present but rarely seen. Many introduced animals have also become established and have played a major part in modifying the forest. Red deer, possums and pigs were liberated in the late 1890s. This area is very popular with both deer and pig hunters. Other imports include rats, mice, cats and stoats. All these animals are regarded as pests due to their destructive influence on vegetation and birdlife.

THINGS TO REMEMBER

DO:

- Stock up with fishing tackle and supplies before heading into this area.
- Check the weather forecast for rainfall, temperatures and wind.
- Take insect repellent, sunscreen, food and a torch (flashlight).
- Move around the river and focus on broken, turbulent water.
- Take a selection of lines and a good variety of flies, particularly dull natural patterns in a range of sizes and weights.
- Take a camera. The scenery and fish are among the most beautiful and wild you are likely to experience anywhere.
- Adjust leader length and fly weight to optimise presentation.

DON'T:

- Attempt night fishing unless you have familiarised yourself with the location in daylight.
- Wander into the native forest without a map and compass.
- Leave anything but your footprints. This is a pristine wilderness zone for everyone, including future generations, to enjoy.
- Light fires, except in designated camping areas.
- Get frustrated if you aren't immediately successful. Take a few deep breaths, relax, and bask in the magnificence of your surroundings. Think of all those people stuck in a traffic jam somewhere in the civilised world.

THINGS TO DO

Explore the Whirinaki Forest Park on guided or unguided walks. A comprehensive network of walks, tracks and huts allows easy access.

- Action and Adventure: Hunting, white-water rafting, kayaking, mountain biking, waterfowl shooting.
- Eco and Nature: Whirinaki Forest Park walks, Lake Waikaremoana Track, tramping, camping.
- Health and Relaxation: Lodges, farm stays, cultural tourism – marae retreats, guided walks.
- Food and Wine: The Covell family produce wines using organic methods. They are open most days for tastings and sales.

Covell Estate Wines Ltd
Troutbeck Road (near Galatea, north-east of Murupara)
Ph: +64-7-366 4827

Maps

Do not head into forested areas in this region without topographical maps and the necessary permits. Topographical Maps 260-V17 (Murupara), 260-V18 (Whirinaki).

Resources

Department of Conservation
Rangitaiki Area Office
State Highway 38
Murupara
Ph: +64-7-366 1080
Fax: +64-7-366 1082
Email: rangitaikiinfo@doc.govt.nz

www.doc.govt.nz
www.whirinakirainforest.info
www.tourism.net.nz/nz/maori-tourism
www.teurewera.com
www.whakatane.com

Fishing

Big Dan Guiding Services
+64-7-366 4579
Email: sara_an@amcom.co.nz

Unparalleled natural beauty.

Boat-based fly anglers on Lake Taupo enjoy a magical morning at the Tongariro Delta.

'Man can learn a lot from fishing – when the fish are biting no problem in the world is big enough to be remembered.'

Orlando A. Battista

TONGARIRO RIVER

5

TONGA (SOUTH WIND); RIRO (CARRIED AWAY) — THIS NAME ORIGINALLY APPLIED TO ALL THREE VOLCANIC PEAKS, TONGARIRO, NGAURUHOE AND RUAPEHU. WHEN NGATORO-I-RANGI WAS IN DANGER OF PERISHING FROM THE COLD ON THE SUMMIT, HE CALLED TO HIS SISTERS IN HAWAIKI FOR FIRE AND HIS WORDS WERE CARRIED ON THE WINGS OF THE SOUTH WIND.

More has been written about the hallowed waters of the Tongariro than any other trout fishery in New Zealand. Tens of thousands of anglers descend on the Lake Taupo region each year to chance their arm on this most famous of waters and the many other superb rivers which flow into New Zealand's largest lake. Despite the significant angling pressure, the Tongariro continues to flourish as the country's most popular river and deservedly maintains its reputation as one of the world's premier fly-fishing destinations.

The fame is certainly not newfound and the river and Lake Taupo fishery have been world acclaimed for well over a hundred years. Certainly, the accolades from overseas fans like the legendary American angler and famous Western writer Zane Grey, who fished here in the 1920s, helped to elevate the Tongariro to mythical status. However, it is the amazing fighting ability of the wild steelhead rainbow trout and the cunning and strength of the trophy size brown trout that continues to draw successive generations back to the banks. A good introduction to the Tongariro for visitors is to see the superb National Trout Centre and hatchery situated on the banks of Tongariro 3 km (1.8 miles) south of Turangi township on State Highway 1.

The Tongariro offers a variety and complexity that few rivers can boast and which only a handful of anglers have the opportunity to fully explore. The flavours of fly fishing are almost boundless, from close encounters with other anglers, isolated wilderness fishing, adventure rafting, drift boating, boat fishing, night fishing, and superb summer dry-fly fishing.

While the other rivers flowing into Lake Taupo provide equally outstanding fishing and each offers its own unique experience, they all deserve individual treatment far outside the scope of this text. (There are several excellent guidebooks available which cover the entire Lake Taupo fishery in detail.) We have singled out the Tongariro as our showcase for the region from our thousands of hours angling here and for the exceptional variety of techniques and conditions available to anglers of all ages and abilities.

The Tongariro is the largest of the rivers feeding the gigantic caldera of Lake Taupo. Born on the snow-capped peaks of the mighty Tongariro National Park volcanoes and charged with run-off from the Kaimanawa Mountains in the east, the river flows over 80 kilometres (50 miles) before passing Turangi township and entering the southern end of the lake. For those with the time and knowledge, the river provides a challenge for all seasons.

Woolly Bugger – a superb wetfly pattern, so effective it is used around the globe. The marabou dressing takes on a pulsing life of its own. Fish dark colours close to the riverbed day or night.

OPPOSITE: The fishing in the Tongariro is world-famous.

Shoulder-to-shoulder wet-fly fishing at dusk at the famous Waitahanui river mouth.

Kaimanawa wilderness section

The headwaters are only open in the summer season and receive little angling pressure. Here the river is sparkling clear, offering remote back-country angling to a relatively small population of large rainbow trout. There are numerous tributary streams flowing off the eastern slopes of the rugged Kaimanawa Forest Park. The main tributary is the Waipakihi River, which flows down a wide shingle valley bordered by the steep bush-clad slopes of the Kaimanawa Mountains. Below Tree Trunk Gorge, the river plummets through a series of spectacular inaccessible gorges. Fishing here is out of the question but there are stunning bush walks and great mountain biking. Try the loop track reached via Tree Trunk Gorge Road off the Desert Road section of State Highway 1, which provides impressive views over the Pillars of Hercules, massive rock towers rising from the river.

Upper reaches

From the hydro dam and Beggs Pool downstream to the Fence Pool there is excellent summer and autumn fishing. There are some bush tracks but the terrain is steep with several gorges and a downstream raft is recommended as the best means of covering this section.

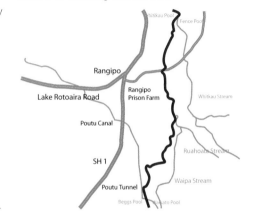

Middle reaches

From the Fence Pool downstream to the State Highway 1 bridge, the Tongariro tumbles through a series of boulder-strewn rapids, reaches and pools as it gradually widens and slows on the journey to the lake. These are the famous sections, which attract the vast majority of anglers targeting the winter runs of rainbow trout entering the river to spawn in the upper reaches. There are over 30 identified pools with interesting names like the Major Jones, Hydro, Admirals and Kamahi; where during peak times anglers will crowd shoulder to shoulder. These sections are still beautifully scenic but do not expect a wilderness experience as there are nearly always other anglers in sight, although this certainly does not detract from the quality of fishing available. Be courteous and take the time to understand the basic etiquette required and you will have a fantastic day with the camaraderie of fellow fly-fishing fanatics from around the globe. There can be crowds but skilled anglers can still fish unhampered in the pocket water between pools and those prepared to walk further from the car parks and main tracks can still experience relative solitude.

Lower reaches

A short distance after flowing under the highway bridge the river's character alters, giving way to a more sedate meandering pace and a very different scenic experience, resembling a large serpentine waterway. There are few rapids in this 8 km (5 mile) section, the water is more discoloured and carves large sigmoid bends through the swampy sediment of the Tongariro flood plain. Near the mouth, the river splits into several forks that flow through a tongue of land before spilling into the lake through separate mouths at the aptly named Delta. This is a popular spot for fly fishing from boats, using high-density sinking lines, smelt imitations and Booby-style flies.

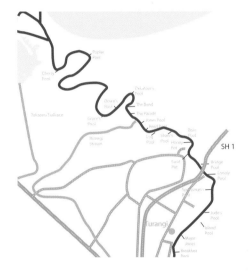

A typical winter scene looking up a section of the famous middle reaches from the banks of the Major Jones Pool with ominous weather moving in over the Kaimanawa Mountains.

Getting There

This is a very easy destination to reach, situated on State Highway 1 in the centre of the North Island. Pull off the highway at the Tongariro River road bridge at Turangi township and you can join the line of anglers plying the famous Bridge Pool just downstream.

The nearest airport is 35 minutes' north at Taupo and there is a small airstrip for light planes on Graces Road five minutes' drive from Turangi. All major bus companies stop in Turangi and this is one of the best places in the country for hitchhikers to thumb a ride. For train enthusiasts and those keen to get a glimpse of the volcanoes, it is possible to take a nostalgic train ride from National Park station.

Access

Wilderness section

The best recommendation for exploring the zone in the Kaimanawa forest is to get fit and pack your tramping boots and camping gear. Like most of New Zealand, the term 'wilderness' means remote, rugged and hard to reach. Those prepared to hike will be rewarded with spectacular scenery,

challenging fly fishing and probably a few blisters. Visitors are advised to seek specific advice from experienced locals or enlist the expertise of a guide. If you have good bush skills, including map reading, and are comfortable in remote back-country environments there are many days of adventurous angling available. This is also a popular area for pursuing sika deer, and some anglers pack both rod and rifle.

Upper

This is a difficult stretch to reach on foot but has some excellent fishing. Contact one of the raft companies in Turangi to arrange day or overnight trips.

Middle

There are well-travelled walking tracks along both banks extending from the State Highway 1 bridge to the upstream winter limits at the Fence Pool – approximately 20 km (12 miles). The Information Centre in Turangi and most of the sports stores have detailed maps showing access roads, tracks and pool names. Alternatively, you can download the map from the DOC website listed in the

Willows frame a
Tongariro fishing spot.

Resources section. There are several access roads and walking tracks off Taupahi Road and State Highway 1, with swing bridges located at the end of Koura Street and below the Red Hut car park providing easy access to the eastern bank.

Lower

There are several kilometres of accessible fishing in the lower river below the road bridge. Vehicle access is via gravel roads at the rear of Turangi township off Tautahanga Road on the downstream left bank and from Graces Road on the true right bank. This section of the river is prone to flooding, has numerous snags and is willow lined, making casting difficult. For those prepared to walk, there is also access to water further downstream on the left bank via Hirangi and Awamate Roads. Uninitiated anglers should ask for information at the local tackle stores or enlist a guide to optimise your experience in these lower sections. The dry-fly and nymph fishing in the summer can be spectacular and there are plenty of large but cagey browns. You can also drive a small boat upriver from the main mouth of the Delta and fish as far as Delatours pool.

Angling

Like all of this region's major rivers, there has been significant change imposed through hydroelectric schemes, farming, forestry and flood protection. However, Mother Nature still plays the lead role in altering the mood of the mighty Tongariro. Many predicted the demise of the fishery with the most recent eruption of Mt Ruapehu in 1995,

The lower river is wide deep water with some excellent fishing and a lot of snags!

which threatened to poison the ecosystem and smother the rock and shingle riverbed. More recently, in 2003, the ravages of the largest flood in a hundred years saw pessimists abandon the fishery and bemoan the disappearance of favourite fishing haunts. We are truly fortunate then that someone forgot to tell the ever-resilient trout. These offspring of stock introduced from California and Scotland have proven their incredible toughness and ability to adapt. Hundreds of thousands of trout continue to navigate through the Tongariro each year to spawn in its tributaries and nurture one of the world's greatest wild fisheries, with trout averaging 1.5 to 3 kg (3.3 to 6.6 lb.), depending on the season. Perhaps, like the fish, we should embrace the ever-changing river conditions and enjoy the challenge of having to adopt new techniques and find new lies when Mother Nature plays her hand.

The entire river is restricted to fly fishing only, including boat fishing in the lower reaches and at the Delta. There is a bag limit of three fish, although catch and release is commonly practised. The size limit is 45 cm (17 in.) and fish in prime condition are excellent eating with firm flesh varying from bright pink to red. Rainbows average around 2 kg (4.4 lb.) and browns around 2.5 kg (5 lb.). However, trophy specimens over 4 kg (8.8 lb.) are landed on a regular basis and very large brown trout over 4.5 kg (10 lb.) can be spotted with careful stalking when the river is running low and clear. They are very wary and difficult to deceive in comparison to their rainbow cousins and few brown trout are captured relative to their population size.

The majority of anglers focus on the winter runs of rainbows heading upstream to spawn. Also, a growing band of fly fishers is now adopting alternative tactics and very successfully targeting fish throughout the year using a variety of styles incorporating dry flies, traditional wets and small nymphs. One especially effective method is Czech-style nymphing, which involves dropping weighted nymphs into fast-flowing pocket water on a very short line.

Due to the river's popularity, all anglers should have a good understanding of river-fishing etiquette. Remember that everyone is there for an enjoyable and memorable experience. The Taupo region offers more water than you could dream to fish in a lifetime; the Tongariro offers a massive expanse of fishable water but it is only one of many superb rivers that feed the lake. Be prepared

A shoal of sizeable rainbows heads up a Tongariro tributary.

to share pools with others and remember the basic maxim: 'the longer the walk, the fewer the people'. All etiquette starts with courtesy and common sense; if in doubt ask, but here are a few basic rules to keep you out of trouble:

- Stop and think! If a pool or stretch of water is already occupied and looks crowded, it probably is. Try walking to the next spot or wait on the bank for your turn.
- Always enter a pool behind any angler already fishing. If you are fishing a wet line downstream, start at the top and work down. Conversely, if you are nymph fishing with a floating line, start at the base of the run and work up. Most pools do not have room to accommodate both downstream and upstream anglers comfortably so find a stretch of river where anglers are fishing the same style as you.
- Keep moving steadily through the pool.
- Don't hog a spot.

- Keep to water where you can cast successfully; some pools are best left for those with expertise with long-distance casts, roll casts or backhand casts.
- Be friendly. Never bust straight into a pool already being fished. Ask the angler(s) fishing or waiting on the banks if you can join in. Most fisher folk are friendly and accommodating.
- If an angler near you hooks a fish, leave them room to play it and allow them to return to their spot after they have landed it.

Season

- Wilderness (above the Waikato Falls): 1 October to 30 June.
- Upper River (above the Fence Pool): 1 December to 31 May.
- Middle, lower reaches and Lake Taupo (below the Fence Pool): open all year round.

There is room and fun to be had by everyone as long as you respect others.

Techniques and Tactics

Traditionally anglers have focused on the winter and autumn seasons, when large runs of rainbow trout in their thousands migrate out of the lake into the river to spawn. Like steelhead and salmon species, these trout return to their birthplace to reproduce. During this period they are primarily focused on sex and not food. However, their feeding instinct and aggressive mating behaviour means they will strike at a wide variety of flies regardless of whether these resemble food or not. Spawning fish generally hug the bottom and the secret to inducing a take is presenting a fly in their territory or lie by bouncing your rig on or very near the bottom. The two most common approaches are to fish a streamer-type wet fly on a sinking line or casting a pair of weighted nymphs upstream on a floating line, using wool or colourful yarn as a strike indicator.

Sinking line

To facilitate long casts and to reach the deeper pockets, the standard wet line adopted for fishing streamers is a fast-sinking shooting head. This is fished in a downstream arch by casting across the river and letting the current naturally swing the fly across the riverbed. An even older style of wet lining that is still very effective when applied in the right spot is to cast or release line directly downstream. Slowly retrieve the fly upstream using a wet line with the appropriate sink rate to get the fly near the bottom, which will be

dictated by the depth of water and velocity of the current. The fly should be literally bouncing across the bottom with the current and the swing of the line providing the enticing lifelike action. You may lose the odd fly to snags but this is where the fish are holding.

Floating line

In the last decade, upstream nymphing has overtaken the more traditional wet-fly approach in popularity. The critical rule when nymphing on the Tongariro is to have enough weight in your nymphs and the correct leader length to reach the bottom quickly. However, the tricky part is that the nymphs still need to be sufficiently light to bounce naturally downstream. If your leader length is correct you should be able to detect the bottom contact by watching your indicator as it floats high on the surface. Any dip, sideways draw or hesitation should be struck quickly.

Anglers adopting a floating-line approach also need to be able to mend the line up or downstream to counter the effects of current on the fly line. You need to mend the line throughout a drift to ensure the indicator and flies are travelling downstream free of line drag. Not all holding water is suitable for nymphing; select water free from back eddies, whirlpools or sections of varying speeds. The least common technique I see on the Tongariro these days is good old-fashioned dry-fly fishing. This is ironic given that in warmer months the Tongariro has

Bead-head nymphs are an ideal weighted pattern for bottom bouncing.

This hen fell for the standard Tongariro winter nymphing rig: a #8 weight-forward floating line, high visibility yarn indicator, a 3 m (9 ft. 9 in.) leader with a weighted bead-head Bomb and a small unweighted Glo Bug.

Alan Martindale takes advantage of rainy conditions on the lower river.

There are many versions and colours of the Glo Bug pattern, which is said to imitate a trout egg. This fly is very effective as both an upstream nymph and fished across and downstream on a wet line.

some of the most reliable evening hatches in the North Island. On any still, balmy evening I can stroll down to the banks of the Major Jones pool to witness a cloud of sedge and caddis-flies with scores of fish rising through the entire pool. Granted, you do need to cover up well and coat all exposed skin with insect repellent to survive the droves of hungry mosquitoes, but for the less hardy there are excellent opportunities in the middle of the day to fish terrestrial dries like cicada or beetle imitations.

Flies and Rigs

If you are targeting migrating rainbow trout with a nymphing outfit, a great starter is the local two-nymph rig with a suitably weighted bead-head Hare and Copper as your 'bomb' and a small unweighted Glo Bug attached as a dropper fly. We keep the nymphs as small as possible but you still need sufficient weight in the lead fly to get the rig quickly to the bottom. Leader length and the weight of flies needs to be carefully adjusted to match the depth and speed of the current; generally a length of 3 to 4 m (9 ft. 9 in. to 13 ft.) of 4 to 6 kg (8.8 to 13 lb.) is sufficient. Tie the smaller point fly about 20 cm (8 in.) directly off the hook bend of the bead-head. This rig results in fewer tangles and is simple to assemble. The high volumes, swift flows, back eddies and deep pools often make it difficult to fish nymphs naturally and newcomers are advised to use a heavier #8 or #9 weight line and rod to accommodate long casts, easier mending and, more importantly, to handle large hard-fighting fish in swift flows!

Wet-fly fishing utilising a sinking line is an older, more traditional approach similar to European salmon-fishing techniques and now coming back into vogue. It is just as effective as nymphing once the technique is mastered and used on appropriate water. This is a great way to methodically sweep the bottom of wider pools difficult to cover with an upstream nymphing outfit. Our staple favourite fly for wet lining is the Woolly Bugger. A variety of colours including olive, dark green, brown, black

A traditional Matuku-style Yellow Rabbit wet fly, just as effective now as a century ago and a fly which has accounted for many large brown trout.

The versatile and highly effective Woolly Bugger. One of our top performing wet-fly patterns.

and even orange have their moments. Our general rule for colours is 'dull day, dull fly' and vice versa. Keep to the smaller flies (sizes 8 to 10 streamer wet-fly hooks) when the river is relatively clear and increase size when the river is running high and dirty. Other proven patterns include Red Setters, Rabbit Flies in yellow, orange and black, and variations of the Fuzzy Wuzzy.

If you want to experiment and cover a variety of techniques, take a full selection of spare spools including fast-sinking, floating and medium-sinking lines. Likewise you can maximise your options if you take a wide selection of wet flies, nymphs, dries and emerger patterns. I even carry a couple of large deer-hair mice flies for skittering across the surface in the back of pools. I was experimenting with one of these monstrosities on the Reed Pool one evening only to have it unceremoniously removed in an explosive surface strike, so I now carry them as a permanent fixture in my fly box.

Tips and Tricks

Regardless of the time of year or river conditions there are always plenty of fish in the Tongariro. The big runs are triggered by steady rainfall creating a fresh or spate, which sparks the trout's spawning instinct to head upstream. The period just before and after peak flows from a period of rain can produce magic fishing and it is not uncommon to see three or four anglers in a pool all hooked up to fresh-run fish in these conditions. If the river is high and discoloured, this is usually a great time to venture out even if it's pouring with rain. When the river is very muddy and high, it is still possible to take fish by dribbling

Which one would you eat? Kelts or slabs – fish that have spawned – should be returned to the water or humanely dispatched when they are in very poor condition.

Anglers fishing the traditional wet fly with fast-sinking shooting-head line.

There can be no mistake identifying a fresh-run Tongariro rainbow in peak condition. They have flanks of silver and clean, sharp, undamaged tails. This fish has just entered the river from the lake to head upstream to spawn.

a wet fly downstream against the banks where trout will be holding in the shallows to escape the main surge. Be extremely careful in high-flow conditions; there is no need to wade.

During spring and early summer increasing numbers of kelts or 'slabs' are moving back downstream towards the lake. These fish have spawned and tend to be in very poor condition – dark, emaciated and fight and taste like a dead sock. Don't be discouraged as there are always plenty of fresh-run silver bullets in the system throughout the year and especially after a good dowsing of rain.

When the river is low and clear, fish can be spotted easily, but with the increased visibility they become harder to deceive and easier to disturb. Switch to fluorocarbon leaders and smaller natural nymphs like Pheasant Tails, Prince Nymph, Stoneflies or Caddis. Tiny traditional wet flies or a wet fly-and-nymph combination fished across and downstream on a sinking line can be very effective in these conditions.

Don't be afraid to experiment. Many of the most successful flies and techniques have been

introduced by visiting anglers or discovered by innovators thinking laterally. We fish the river a lot at night with wet flies or dries and emerger patterns in the warmer months. After dark you have all the water to yourself and the fish are often very aggressive after a respite from the daytime bombardment of fly lines and flies. This is a prime time to target the big brown trout that are active nocturnal feeders. Always fish with a companion and do not wade deep; the Tongariro has claimed many lives and there is no need to take risks at a time when fish are moving into the shallows to feed. When the fishing is hot you can expect plenty of hits. I managed 11 rainbows in a recent evening session, fish that were all taken on a variety of wet flies, dries and emerger patterns. Always be prepared for an exceptional fish, so use at least 4.5 kg (10 lb.) monofilament and have 200 m (218 yards) of backing.

Equipment and Apparel
The standard Tongariro outer uniform for the chilly winter season is neoprene waders, a waterproof parka or coat and a good thick hat

The Tongariro
winter uniform,
layered for comfort
and safety, complete
with sunglasses for
both sun safety and
protection from
trout flies.

and a gallon of highly potent insect repellent. On still, cloudy days and during and after sunset, mosquitoes will drive you mad and force a retreat if you're not fully protected.

Sunglasses or safety glasses are a must to protect your eyes from fishing flies. It only takes one misdirected cast or a gust of wind to lose your eyesight. Landing nets are useful in many spots where fish cannot be easily beached and a wading staff is handy if your experienced enough to wade deep or attempt river crossings.

Flora and Fauna

The headwaters of the Tongariro lie in the Kaimanawa Mountains, amid the Kaimanawa Forest Park that encompasses a vast expanse of native forest, scrublands and tussock grasslands. The climate in this area is often extreme – hot and dry during summer, with snow and heavy frosts during winter.

Red and silver beech forest covers most of the park. Towards the west giant podocarp forests with rimu, matai and totara become more prominent. At higher altitudes over 1000 m (3280 ft.), the forest gives way to tussock grassland and subalpine vegetation.

The park is a sanctuary for many native birds, the most common being New Zealand pigeons (kereru), fantails, bellbirds, riflemen, New Zealand robins, grey warblers, tomtits, whiteheads and red and yellow-crowned parakeets (kakariki). Also present but in fewer numbers are blue ducks (whio), New Zealand falcon, pipits, tui, moreporks, fernbirds, kakas, and black and pied shags. If you are very lucky you may still hear a kiwi's night call but they are rarely sighted. All birdlife and vegetation in the forest park is protected.

There are both red and sika deer in the park, wild pigs and plenty of hares and rabbits. The sika territory is mainly in the north and east while there are more red deer in the southern and central areas. Possums are a major pest throughout the park and continue to thrive despite ongoing poisoning and trapping efforts.

Anything will work! A Tongariro nymphing fly box full of the weird, wonderful and exotic.

that covers your ears – to protect them from frostbite and low-flying weighted nymphs! It is not uncommon to have sub-zero temperatures and snow; conditions can get particularly unpleasant when the freezing southerly winds funnel down the river. It pays to have plenty of quality warm clothing including fleeces, gloves and warm woollen socks. As with all cold-climate apparel, the secret is to layer, for extreme weather start with polypropylene, followed by fleece and a wind and waterproof outer combined with 7 mm (approximately one-fifth inch) neoprene waders will keep you snug in the worst of blizzards.

Conversely, in the summer, particularly in the upper and lower reaches, the most comfortable outfit is sturdy boots, shorts, a long-sleeved shirt, wide-brimmed hat, plenty of quality sunscreen

A trophy Tongariro brown trout taken on a dark wet fly in the dead of night.

THINGS TO REMEMBER

DO:

- Wear a wading belt around your waders for safety. The Tongariro is a big swift river and has seen too many tragic wading accidents. Belts help trap air and prevent water filling the leggings.
- Release fish if they are not healthy fat specimens. If possible leave the fish in the water and unhook it without touching it.
- Support fish gently upright in the current until they regain energy to swim away.

DON'T:

- Night fish on the river without previous experience on that stretch. Always fish with a companion at night.
- Gut or fillet fish on the riverbanks. Other anglers don't need to put up with your mess or the water rats it attracts.
- Wade before fishing your feet first. Many anglers on the Tongariro wade unnecessarily deep. This invariably disturbs fish and cuts down the angling options for others.

THINGS TO DO

The Tongariro River, Turangi and surrounding countryside offer endless adventure activities. The whole Taupo region is also a golfer's paradise; Wairakei International Golf Course is one of the country's premier courses and one of seven in the area including the Turangi course just south of the township on State Highway 1. Turangi is also renowned as a base for white-water rafting and kayaking on the Tongariro, Rangitikei, Mohaka and Ngaruroro Rivers in the Kaimanawa Forest Park.

- Action and Adventure: Hunting, fishing, mountain biking, hiking or leisurely bush walks, white-water rafting, kayaking, horse trekking, four-wheel-drive biking, wildfowl shooting, rockclimbing and indoor climbing walls, sailing.
- Eco and Nature: Farm visits, wetland bird watching, farm and forest walks.

- Health and Relaxation: Golf, thermal pools and walks, guided and unguided nature walks, lake tours, sightseeing.
- Arts and Gardens: Garden tours, arts and crafts markets, galleries, museums.
- Food and Wine: Cafés and restaurants.
- Shows and Events: Crater to Lake and Tongariro Mountain Classic Multi Sport events, Great Lake Cycle Challenge.

Maps

A topographical map and compass is essential when adventuring into the Kaimanawa Forest Park and headwaters of the Tongariro. Topographical Map 260-T19 (Tongariro) and 260-T20 (Ruapehu).

Resources

Turangi Visitor Centre
Ngwaka Place, Turangi
Ph: +64-7-386 8999
Fax: +64-7-386 8999
Email: turangivc@laketauponz.com

National Trout Centre
State Highway 1
Turangi
Ph: +64-7-386 8085
Email: troutcentre@reap.org.nz

Department of Conservation
Tongariro/Taupo Conservancy
Turanga Place
Turangi
Ph: +64-7-386 8607
Fax: +64-7-386 7086
Email: tpoinfo@doc.govt.nz

www.laketauponz.com
www.laketaupo.co.nz/turangi.htm
www.doc.govt.nz/Explore/Hunting-and-Fishing/Taupo-Fishery
www.tourism.net.nz
www.aatravel.co.nz
www.kiwitourism.com
www.newzealand.com

Blanketed in snow, the three active volcanoes in the heart of the national park, Tongariro (foreground), Ngauruhoe and Ruapehu.

'I really fished mainly
because I wanted to be alone
on the middle of a lake.'

Susan A. Toth

LAKE OTAMANGAKAU

OTAMANGAKAU — THE SENTIMENTAL HEART OF A MAN

6

The 'Big O', as it has become affectionately known by its champions, is paradoxically a comparatively small shallow lake of 150 hectares (370 acres) but the nickname really arose from the size of the lake's fish and the fact that visitors have difficulty pronouncing Otamangakau. By no means a secret spot, this man-made lake was created during the massive hydroelectric power project on the Central Plateau in 1972. This is one of those waters that receives a veritable pilgrimage of devoted anglers each year and has grown in stature to almost mythical status among both local and overseas anglers as a world-class still-water fishery.

Located a short 25-minute drive from the southern end of Lake Taupo, the lake is nestled in an exposed subalpine basin of tussock, scrub and exotic pine forest beneath the forested slopes of Mt Kakaramea and with the brooding volcanic slopes of Mt Tongariro in the near distance.

First-time visitors might mistake the lake for a murky swamp pond, tucked in a nondescript setting, especially when compared to the stunning grandeur of the Tongariro National Park scenery minutes up the road. But don't be fooled by appearances, this fishery has a well-deserved reputation for producing trophy rainbow and brown trout over the magic 4.5 kg (10 lb.) mark and every season attracts anglers from across the globe. This could be attributed partly to the ease of access via sealed roads, but even the diehard back-country aficionado would be hard pressed to argue with the superb quality of fish that the lake can produce at times. On a clear day the scenic consolation to anglers is casting against the backdrop of a towering snow-capped active volcano with the steam vents of the Ketetahi hot springs puffing ominously in the distance.

The lake has three main arms that all fish well under the right conditions, although fluctuating lake levels and heavy weed growth especially in the summer months require a flexible approach to selecting spots. The main inflow from the south-west is from the Te Whaiau Dam via the Otamangakau Canal, which itself fishes well especially after solid rainfall. Water flows out into the Wairehu Canal at the end of the north-eastern arm and flows into the nearby Lake Rotoaira, another larger, highly productive and distinctively different fishery in its own right.

Getting There

Otamangakau is conveniently situated in the centre of the North Island and you can drive directly to the lake edge either travelling north or south on State Highway 1 or from the west off State Highway 4. The nearest town with well-stocked tackle stores and supplies for the traveller is Turangi at the south end of Lake Taupo on the

Simmon's Attractor – a local Turangi pattern. Very effective in the heat of summer as a generic imitation of large flying insects like cicadas.

OPPOSITE: Fishing the depths of Lake Otamangakau.

Blue skies with cotton-wool clouds.

banks of the famous Tongariro River. From Turangi the most scenic route is via State Highway 41 over the Te Ponanga Saddle Road winding straight into the National Park through mature native forest and providing magnificent views of Mt Pihanga, Lake Rotoaira and Mt Tongariro.

If you are heading northbound on State Highway 1 take the Rangipo turn-off onto State Highway 47, or if you are on State Highway 4 turn off at National Park township and drive east across the base of the glorious Mt Ruapehu.

From State Highway 47 take the access road marked with a triple signpost Wanganui Intake, Otamangakau Dam, and Te Wairehu Dam. Follow the sign for the boat ramp if you're launching a vessel. There is another lake access and a basic boat ramp down the gravel road signposted Wairehu Control Gate also off State Highway 47, but for newcomers we recommend the sealed

route, which also provides more options for the shore-based angler.

Access

Many anglers choose to use boats, float tubes and canoes, which certainly opens up more options. However, the shore fishing can still provide excellent sport for those willing to walk, stalk and wade. When lake levels rise, the shoreline access becomes more difficult, but there are always plenty of spots to flick a fly over the weed banks and the canal provides several kilometres of easy walking. Watercraft can reach most corners of the lake but aquatic weed can make life difficult, especially during the prime summer season. While the majority of fish are taken by those on the water, the skilled and fit shore-based angler can expect great sport fishing in the shallows that are less accessible to the boat angler. We always take our waders in the boat and will convert to shore fishing if the deeper channels and holes are not producing.

Angling

The 'Big O' lies near a wide range of world-class trout waters, including the mighty Lake Taupo and its feeder streams, the back-country streams of the Kaimanawa Mountains and the exceptional dry-fly fishing available on the rivers flowing off the northern and eastern slopes of Mt Ruapehu. But it is the unique environment in the lake itself that distinguishes this fishery from many of these other outstanding waters. The water is not crystal clear but instead remains discoloured year round and aquatic weed grows prolifically across the entire lake. It is this ecosystem that creates the huge abundance of insect life, which in turn creates the staggering growth rates in both the rainbow and brown trout. On a warm summer's day the lake can turn on an incredible

smorgasbord of trout delicacies including damsels, mayflies, caddis, snails, dragonflies, midges, blood worms and terrestrials like cicadas, beetles and even mice. Unlike most other Taupo fisheries there are no smelt present and so the insect-based nature of the lake requires the angler to adopt a very different approach.

Such is the importance and popularity of this fishery that the Department of Conservation (DOC) has been closely monitoring the lake since 1994 in an attempt to better understand the dynamics of the trout population with the hope of optimising the trophy potential. There is a good stock of both browns and rainbows averaging around 2.5 kg (5 lb.). Many of these fish are able to survive several spawning seasons and continue to grow with the prodigious food source.

While DOC research suggests the odds of catching a trophy fish is lower than during the boom times of the 1980s and mid-1990s, and the fishery struggled to produce the same number of

Why it's worth a visit. Kent with a beautiful trophy in superb condition.

A guide and client in action.

Season

Open 1 October to 31 May. There is a bag limit of one fish per angler; however, catch and release is strongly encouraged. A Taupo licence is required but if you would like to fish the nearby Lake Rotoaira, which is privately owned, you must obtain an additional permit available from the Rotoaira Fishing Camp, located on the southern shore off State Highway 47.

Techniques and Tactics

One of the advantages of the 'Big O' is that just about every fly-fishing technique will catch fish at certain times. The key to consistent success is to be fishing the right technique at the right time. Due to the abundance of food, the fish can become very selective and fickle and the successful angler is generally the one who is constantly observing and prepared to change and improvise.

The majority of fly anglers concentrate their efforts on nymph fishing with floating lines on the edge of weed banks and channels. Leader length needs to match the depth of water and the weight of nymphs selected. Depending on where the fish are feeding in the water column, flies can be anything from unweighted to lightly weighted and with the wary nature of these fish leaders of 4 to 6 m (13 to 19.5 ft.) with fluorocarbon tippets down to 2.5kg (5lb.) will often solicit more strikes. We often use a small white yarn indicator with a two-nymph rig and vary the presentation between dead drifting the flies and slow retrieve. If there is surface activity or a good number of cicadas or dragonflies, try switching to a tandem rig with a large terrestrial dry fly and nymph suspended subsurface. There's nothing more depressing than having a hungry monster attack your hookless indicator, so why not use a big ugly visible dry fly as a substitute!

A less common but equally successful approach, especially where wind conditions are creating a bow or drag on a floating line, is to cast and retrieve nymphs or wet flies on a slow or

trophy trout (over 4.5 kg or 10 lb.) during the late 1990s, it continues to remain healthy and, like all ecosystems, population dynamics will invariably fluctuate over time.

The good news for anglers is the trophy population appears to be on the increase after reaching a low point in 1999–2000. Flooding in the post-spawning season of 1998 may have been responsible for killing many adult kelts that would normally have survived and grown to larger sizes. Despite this, the lake is not generally kind to the casual visitor and even in boom years the catch rate for the hours of effort is low. Even seasoned veterans and professional guides will experience blank days and most trophy fish represent many hours of effort and learning.

Remember, this is a small fragile fishery; DOC trapping and survey research indicates that the majority of large fish are likely to have been caught at least once previously. The key to the trophy fishery is that fish continue to survive and grow, which makes catch and release imperative if the quality of the fishery is to be maintained. If anglers kill fish or practise poor catch-and-release techniques, it will have a major impact on this fishery.

medium-sinking line. Vary the depth and retrieve rate to find where the fish are holding and keep trying different patterns. A small Hamill's Killer with a Bloodworm nymph behind can be lethal or try a Damselfly pattern in conjunction with a claret Woolly Bugger. If neither of these techniques is working, try hard on the bottom in the deeper holes and channels between the weed banks. This is a good option if there is little obvious fish movement in the shallows or on the surface. We usually employ a high-density fast-sinking, shooting-head line for ease of casting, but any sinking line will do provided it has sufficient density to drag a buoyant fly to the bottom. Proven deep-fished patterns include a brown, green or black Booby Fly on an ultra-slow retrieve or a floating snail imitation left untouched near the bottom.

The predominant south-westerly wind can howl across this basin, making life uncomfortable, but the versatile and well-equipped angler can still hunt effectively by moving to a more sheltered arm of the lake or by changing from a floating line to a slow sinker. Conversely, warm balmy days can provide ideal casting conditions

Watersnails thrive on the weed banks.

and in the summer months (December to March) there can be some huge hatches of insects with the air and water becoming thick with damsels, dragonflies and cicadas. Unfortunately, this does not necessarily translate into easier fishing and many frequent visitors have witnessed the lake coming alive with fish sipping and rolling on the surface frantically feeding but, infuriatingly, ignoring every artificial fly offered.

You need to be adaptable and patient to fool the 'Big O' fish and one of the central rules to our approach is to spend a lot of time on the water. Arrive in the morning and fish until evening; at

Well-maintained concrete ramps make launching easy.

Another victim of the Bloodworm.

specimen floated past frantically trying to escape the surface film but only succeeded in sending out concentric panic rings of water. Adam was slowly knitting in his first cast as I mumbled about our poor fly selection given the obvious insect fest going on around us. An abrupt lift of the rod and a somersaulting rainbow silenced me; five minutes later Adam had landed and released a chubby 3 kg (6.6 lb.) hen.

Firing out my first cast I was reflecting on this uncharacteristic luck and pessimistically mused over the probability of another strike within the next dozen casts. Twitching the line to start the flies moving I was completely unprepared for the savage grab that ripped the line from my grasp and had the reel screaming with backing fast disappearing into the nearby weed. The fish fought stubbornly and circled deep under the stern trying to find refuge and it was a nervous 10-minute struggle at maximum pressure before the fish surfaced. Not until I lifted the net over the gunwale did we realise the magnificent condition of this fat 4.5 kg (10 lb.) hen, certainly one of the best-conditioned fish I had captured. Not a great deal of time was available for reflection on this beautiful trophy fish as Adam struck yet another fish, which we promptly landed.

some stage the fish will come on the bite. I remember a sunny February day when Adam and I made a last-minute decision to fish the 'Big O'. We didn't leave Turangi until mid morning and by the time we launched the boat at midday the lake was already busy with anglers keenly plying every arm of the lake. We drifted from the ramp in the light breeze while we rigged our rods and rather than start the motor and disturb the tranquillity of the day we simply dropped the anchor over the first weed bank we passed. Adam fired a pair of nymphs out under an indicator while I tied on a size-14 Bloodworm on a slow-sinking line, despite the swarms of damselflies buzzing around us. The monotonous clatter of cicadas was almost deafening and the occasional

Three fish from the 'Big O' in less than half an hour is certainly not a feat I would like to gamble on repeating, but it just shows what can happen when the fish turn on. It turned out to be a very special afternoon, the lake was simply on fire and we were privileged to see several excellent fish landed by other anglers, including a magnificent 5.2 kg (11.5 lb.) trophy captured and released from a float tube by a regular visitor from Colorado.

Flies and Rigs

This is a very difficult lake to prescribe any particular rig or confine yourself to just a couple of flies. We eventually agreed upon a size-14 Bloodworm and size-12 Snail as our favourite picks, but I would feel ill-equipped without at least a dozen patterns in varying sizes and

A 5.2-kg (11.5 lb.) smile!

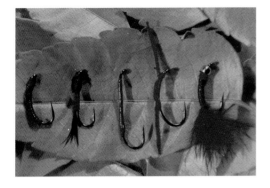

FAR LEFT: Bloodworm imitations. The painted hook is a personal favourite.

LEFT: Try a swimming Damsel as your lead fly.

colours. Always fish two distinctly different patterns to cover your options. Try a small black nymph combined with a plastic ribbed Bloodworm on either a floating or slow-sinking line. One of the favoured imitations is a Damsel nymph and I often fish these in shades of olive and brown as a lead fly with a smaller nymph as a point fly. You can use up to three flies but our experience is that fish tend to bust off with more than two due to the prolific net weed.

Tips and Tricks

Take a well-stocked fly box and keep experimenting with flies until you crack the code on the day. The fish will often be feeding selectively and even with an abundance of winged or emerging insects, the fish might favour a snail or bloodworm imitation fished mid water or near the bottom. If you're using a boat, float tube or canoe keep varying your approach and move positions. Sometimes anchoring with the bow in a weed bank and the stern hanging over the channel, with a second back anchor to prevent the vessel swinging, will provide frequent bites if fish are regularly cruising the weed edges.

At other times, random drifting and casting to sighted fish or working the wind lanes on a breezy day will be the key. Some of the best brown-trout fishing is in the knee-deep shallows and fish are often spotted by their distinctive bow wakes as they pursue their prey. Use large Cicada or Dragonfly dry flies; if the fish don't like them drifted dead then twitch or skate the fly,

but hold on tight. Have plenty of backing on your reel as some of these fish will take off like steam trains and accounts of reels being spooled are not uncommon.

The night fishing can be spectacular but this is only recommended if you have a good knowledge of the lake. Mosquitoes and sandflies can make life miserable if you are not protected.

Equipment and Apparel

On warmer days the margins can be waded comfortably in shorts and a T-shirt. Polaroid glasses, a broad-rimmed hat and sunscreen are essential. Summer conditions are often scorching hot and there is very little natural shade or shelter. If the lake level is high the margins will be sodden and swampy so waders are useful, although weed banks pose a nuisance for the land-based angler.

This is a great location for float tubes, float boats and paddleboats, and we have seen many strange vessels of all shapes and sizes used to good effect. These vessels provide both mobility and stealth and have accounted for a fair share of trophy fish.

Other useful items in a boat include a depth sounder for pinpointing drop-offs and holes and a large-rimmed deep-bodied landing net (you don't want to be the angler providing the day's amusement trying to fit a large trout into a small net only to have it flop over the rim to freedom). Even better are landing nets with built-in weigh scales in the handle, which allow you to quickly record and release your prize.

Flora and Fauna

The Tongariro National Park covers 82,000 hectares and was formally created by Parliament in 1894; it is New Zealand's and one of the world's oldest national parks. The initiative came from Te Heuheu Tukino, chief of the Ngati Tuwharetoa Maori tribe that settled in an area comprising the northern parts of the present park. At the park's centre are three active volcanoes: Tongariro, Ngauruhoe and Ruapehu. Ruapehu is the main skiing mountain in the North Island, but its snow-capped appearance camouflages the active volcano within. Crater Lake at the top of this mountain, although too hot and acidic to swim in, is an awesome spectacle.

Vegetation in the park is influenced by a number of factors, including altitude, Taupo pumice soils, fire, erosion, grazing by herbivores and rainfall distribution. There is a diverse range of habitats, ranging from remnants of rainforest to barren glaciers. From the lowest altitudes to 1000 m (3280 ft.) there are still abundant tracts

of mixed podocarp-broadleaf rainforest filled with ferns, orchids and fungi. At higher altitudes, beech forest occurs and scrublands and tussock land cover extensive areas in the north-west and around Mt Ruapehu. The highest levels in the park are dominated by scree slopes and stone fields, which are very unstable.

The vertebrate fauna is primarily birds, although native mammals are represented by short-tailed and long-tailed bats. More than 56 bird species live in or visit the park, including vulnerable species such as brown kiwi, kaka, blue duck (whio) and North Island fernbird. The native fauna, however, has been seriously depleted by species introduced prior to 1922. These include rat, stoat and cat as predators, and herbivores such as rabbit, hare, brush-tailed possum and red deer, which are the target of constant eradication projects.

Lake Otamangakau itself attracts a large variety of waterfowl and is popular with duck shooters during the closed fishing season.

THINGS TO REMEMBER

DO:

- Be prepared to work hard and put in the hours.
- Keep a close eye on the weather. The national park with its large volcanic mountains and altitude above sea level has an unpredictable climate. It's not uncommon to have stifling heat one day followed by near-freezing temperatures the next. Always check the weather forecast and seek information from local DOC offices or from Turangi, Ohakune or National Park village.
- Take insect repellent, sunscreen and food.
- Take a good selection of fly sizes; nymphs should be non-weighted or very lightly weighted. Start with small sizes and sparsely dressed patterns (nymph sizes 10 to 16).
- Remove all weed from vessels and equipment when leaving the lake.
- Take a second anchor if boat fishing. Dropped from the stern it will reduce boat spin in windy conditions.

DON'T:

- Give up! The 'Big O' can switch on just as fast as it shuts off.
- Anchor too close to other anglers. Even on busy days there is plenty of lake and many holes, weed banks and channels to explore.
- Forget some weigh scales or even better a landing net with built-in weigh scales. Some anglers also like to quickly take measurements and a photo to record condition factors before releasing their prize. There is no need to kill fish to have a trophy wall mount. Taxidermists can create excellent replicas of your prize using measurements and good photographs.

THINGS TO DO

You are already in the heart of one of the world's most majestic volcanic playgrounds so after you've been outsmarted by some 'Big O' fish take a tour and enjoy the scenery. In winter North Island's two largest ski-fields, Turoa and Whakapapa (both on Mt Ruapehu) open for business, offering top skiing and facilities.

- Action and Adventure: Other options in the national park include mountain biking, kayaking, hunting, mountain climbing and abseiling. Both hot and cold springs are found around the park with silica rapids and waterfalls. This area hosts excellent camping, trekking, hunting, fishing and bush walks. The Tongariro Crossing is one of New Zealand's most popular day tramps taking in a range of beautiful vistas. You do need to have a reasonable degree of fitness, proper tramping equipment and good weather for this challenge. Another classic adventure activity ranked among New Zealand's best mountain bike trails is the '42 Traverse' running through the Tongariro forest.
- Eco and Nature: Farm visits, bush walks, Department of Conservation tours, horse trekking, four-wheel-drive tours biking.
- Health and Relaxation: Visit or stay at the Grand Chateau on the slopes of Ruapehu if you like to be pampered and travel in style.

Maps

Lake Otamangakau is not a hard place to find and a good New Zealand road map is perfect if you've just come to fish the lake. For those intrepid travellers seeking adventures throughout the Tongariro National Park we recommend Topographical Maps 260-T19 (Tongariro), 260-T19 (Ruapehu) and 260-S20 (Ohakune).

Resources

Department of Conservation
Whakapapa Visitor Centre
Whakapapa Village
Mt Ruapehu
Ph: +64-7-892 3729
Fax: +64-7-892 3814
Email: whakapapavc@doc.govt.nz
Walks, flora, fauna and volcanology information and displays.

Ruapehu Information Centre – Ohakune
Clyde Street, Ohakune
Ph: +64-6-385 4189
Fax: +64-6-385 8527
Email: info@ruapehudc.govt.nz
Web: www.ruapehu.tourism.co.nz

Ruapehu Alpine Lifts (Ruapehu skiing)
Customer Service offices:
Whakapapa: Ph: +64-7-892 3738
Turoa: Ph: +64-6-385 8456
Web: www.mtruapehu.com

www.newzealand.com
www.visitruapehu.com
www.alpinescenictours.co.nz

A top-condition Tekapo river fish ready for release.

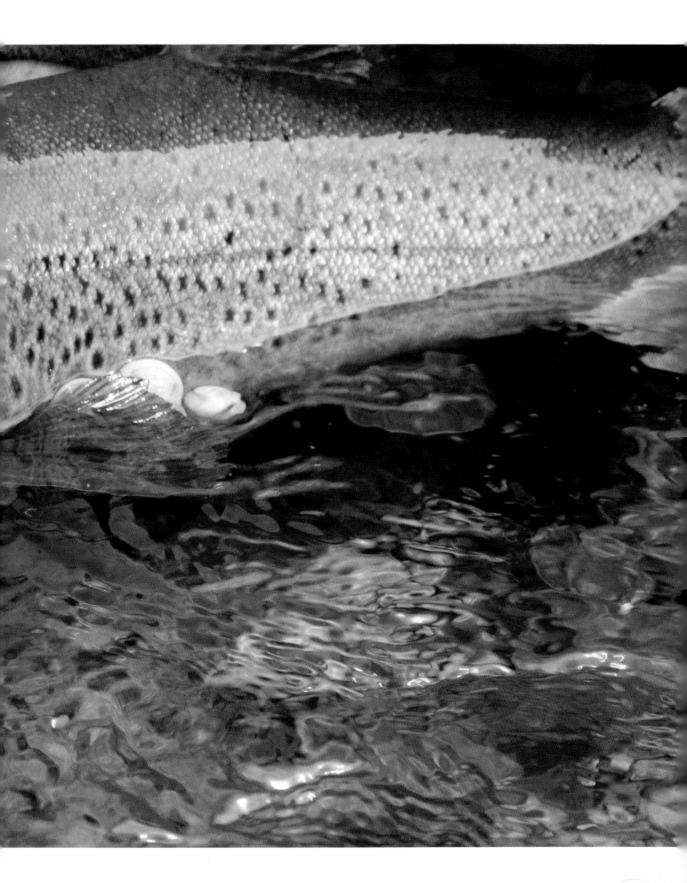

'Fishing is a delusion entirely surrounded by liars in old clothes.'
Don Marquis

HURUNUI RIVER

7

HURU (HAIR); NUI (BIG) – ONE EXPLANATION IS THE NAME MEANS FLOWING HAIR, AND THE RIVER
DOES HAVE SOMETHING OF THIS APPEARANCE WHEN LOOKING DOWN ON IT FROM THE FOOTHILLS.

One of the gems of the Canterbury region, the Hurunui River begins life on the eastern slopes of the mighty Southern Alps just above Lake Sumner. This is an expansive river system that offers an abundance of quality fly-fishing opportunities and is highly regarded by local enthusiasts. The river flows west to east and enters the Pacific Ocean at Pegasus Bay, 120 km (77 miles) north of Christchurch on the east coast of the South Island.

Typical of many of the larger east-coast rivers, the Hurunui constantly evolves and changes character in relatively short distances as it tumbles down the steep gradients of the Alps and then meanders across the Canterbury Plains. In the headwaters the tributaries are swift flowing, crystal clear and shallow. The water races through majestic beech forests and high-country tussock lands. In this region the river has a main branch and a south branch that diverts around a high mountain promontory. From the confluence of these branches the new combined flow cuts around the base of the Glynn Wye Range and becomes a more concentrated, powerful river. These middle sections are deep with stable rapids and pools interspersed with sections of gorge carved in the bedrock where adventurous anglers can still reach plenty of prime spots. Around Balmoral Forest the river exits the gorge and separates into several shingle braids before it hits the sea.

Getting There

The Hurunui River system is one of the most accessible brown-trout and salmon fisheries in the South Island, being within easy driving distance of central Christchurch. There are regular daily flights from the North Island and a handful of international flights into Christchurch. The middle reaches around Hawarden are 120 km (77 miles) from Christchurch and a campervan or rental car can have you casting a fly within two hours. We arrived on an early-morning flight from Auckland and after collecting our campervan, managed to do our grocery shopping, visit our favourite tackle store, take a few wrong turns and still land our first brownie before lunch. For those on a more generous budget or hunting trophy fish, a local guide is well worth the money and can arrange four-wheel-drive or helicopter access.

Access

Vehicle access is via Lake Sumner Road, which runs off State Highway 7 and can be reached via Hawarden if you are heading north from Christchurch. Signposts clearly mark the route upriver and at this point normal two-wheel drive road vehicles are fine. The sealed road leads onto a winding gravel access road as it heads into the

The Green Humpy – sometimes called a Green Wulff. Exceptionally good as a summer fly when lots of terrestrial insects are in the air.

OPPOSITE: Sparkling water on the upper Hurunui.

Swing bridge river crossing.

gorge. There are several access points for anglers, which are clearly marked by Fish and Game Council signposts. After about 25 km (15.6 miles) you reach the Sisters Swing Bridge and a livestock gate. A good walking track leads both up and down the river from this point, offering access to several kilometres of fishable riverbank. A little further on you reach the scenic Lake Taylor, which marks the upper limit for conventional vehicles. The station track beyond this gate is suitable only for four-wheel-drive vehicles and provides access to Lake Sumner where there are huts to stay in. Note there is only limited access to this region and the gate is locked. For information on access contact Department of Conservation in Christchurch (see Resources section).

The upper Hurunui region is a true back-country location, some of which can be accessed by four-wheel-drive, or anglers can enlist the use

of helicopters and fishing guides. However, there is nothing preventing the fit and experienced angler from tramping in on foot, although the terrain is fairly steep.

Angling

Brown trout and quinnat salmon are both found in the Hurunui River. Resident brown trout can be found year round with the period from December through March considered the most productive. Trout average around 2 kg (4.4 lb.) but there are good trophy fish in the over 4 kg (8.8 lb.) range in more remote areas. As with many back-country rivers, catch and release is strongly encouraged in the upper reaches. Try to handle the fish as little as possible and cradle in the current until they have recovered sufficiently to swim away. Salmon start running from late November onwards with the peak of the run around February and March. The majority of salmon anglers target fresh-run fish at the mouth and in the lower reaches with spinning tackle, although more and more diehard fly anglers are now pursuing these elusive quinnat which reach up to 15 kg (33 lb.).

Catch and release is encouraged.

Season

The fishery is divided into three sections, each with different bag limits and open seasons for trout and salmon.

- Headwaters, North Branch – above Lake Sumner: 1 December to 31 March. Bag limit is two trout and two salmon.
- Western Zone – above the main and South Branch confluence: trout season 1 October to 30 April, salmon season 1 October to 28 February. Bag limit two trout and two salmon.
- Eastern Zone – middle and lower reaches: open all year round for trout and 1 October to 30 April for salmon. Bag limit four trout and two salmon.

You don't have to move far from your vehicle to experience superb fishing.

Mist at first light on Lake Taylor.

Techniques and Tactics

The majority of fly anglers concentrate their efforts on dry-fly and nymph fishing to sighted fish or likely holding water. Anglers need to be prepared to walk significant distances between good fish-holding water; as with many rivers much of the bottom is barren and the more water covered generally increases the chances of finding productive pockets. We covered around 20 km (12.5 miles) one day and found

Be prepared to walk for your fish. The team on the march with full angling and camera equipment.

the fish stacked up in short stretches of river with nothing for two or three kilometres in between. The upside is that the terrain in the Hurunui watershed is generally easy to hike, with good access to riverbanks and unimpeded casting in most spots. Take extra care with river crossings; some patches of riverbed can be prone to slime and algae especially in low water conditions.

Brown trout in this system are typical of high-country fish in the Canterbury region, demonstrating opportunistic feeding behaviour, and they are usually not overly selective. Careful stalking, placement of cast and the size of fly are more critical than the type of pattern. Keep to the smaller nymphs below size 12 and be prepared to

switch patterns and weights to entice strikes. Our experiences of individual fish varied considerably, with those fish not feeding proving extremely difficult to entice unless the fly was placed on its nose, whereas those fish actively prowling could be quite suicidal.

In the middle reaches where the river runs through a series of gorges, anglers are well advised to fish into the late afternoon and evening as there can be a superb caddis hatch often lasting into darkness. Fishing down and across with caddis imitations such as Goddard Caddis and Elk Hair Caddis can provoke explosively aggressive strikes from feeding trout. Small wet flies also perform well when fished

FAR LEFT: Al Troth's classic Elk Hair Caddis.

LEFT: A blue Blowfly Humpy, another deadly Hurunui dry fly.

in this situation. Upstream of the Sisters Swing Bridge it pays to fish small nymphs under an indicator in the deeper pools that often hold unsighted fish. Anglers taking on the challenge of the wily Hurunui brown trout need to be well equipped. Casting needs to be accurate and powerful as the dreaded Canterbury north-westerly wind often howls through the valley during the prime summer months. The intrepid angler will need the ability to punch a large attractor dry fly or pair of weighted nymphs into a strong wind and land them delicately enough so as not to frighten the fish, which may often be sitting in less than a metre (39 in.) of water. Fly rods suited to #6 weight lines and matched with weight-forward floating lines are recommended for this style of fishing.

Long leaders will catch more fish. We used very long leaders of over 5 m (16 ft.) constructed from Poly leaders, tapered monofilament and 2 to 4 kg (4.4 to 8.8 lb.) fluorocarbon tippets. The tapered leader acts more as an extension of the fly line and allows casts to be fired into high winds and still roll out straight to cover fish without frightening them with the fly line.

In general, the upper and middle reaches are best sight fished, although all likely spots are worth a cast, especially the fast white water in the head of pools and runs, which will often hide a feeding fish. There is no doubt that a sharp

pair of eyes and quality Polaroid sunglasses pay dividends, as a mere shadow or flick of a tail is often all that can be seen when fish are not rising.

Flies and Rigs

Our favourite two flies for the Hurunui River are a size-12 Pheasant and Peacock nymph with a black tungsten bead for weight and a large size-10 Humpy dry fly. If fish are feeding or resting hard on the bottom, fish the Pheasant and Peacock in a tandem rig with another generic nymph pattern such as a Hare and Copper. Alternatively, if fish are feeding actively on the surface or subsurface, suspend the nymph about 1 m (39 in.) under the dry fly. Other good dry patterns include Daddy Longlegs, Goddard Caddis, and Royal Wulff.

Tips and Tricks

Beware the dreaded north-westerly foehn (warm, dry) winds. North Island and offshore anglers will need to adapt both their rigs and casting styles to cope with the curse of Canterbury. Gusts during the heat of summer days will reach over 30 knots and anglers will more often than not be contending with head winds over 10 knots. Tapered leaders are essential and casts should be kept short and crisp with a high backcast and positive downward forward cast. Paradoxically, the fishing can improve with wind as the angler

Magic moments: the capture and release of a beautiful Hurunui brown.

Attaching a long leader before launching the assault.

becomes less visible and more terrestrial food is blown onto the water. When the wind is gusting, try to time your cast between gusts and keep false casts to a minimum.

Equipment and Apparel

Come prepared for some serious hiking and carry a selection of clothing layers as weather conditions can change quickly, especially when the cold southerly winds sweep into the valleys. High-quality tramping boots combined with polypropylene leggings and quick-drying synthetic shorts provide excellent protection from both the insects and the elements. Be prepared to get wet. Moving between banks will increase the number of fish spotted and allow anglers to optimise sunlight directions. Waders are not recommended, as they are not comfortable for long hikes and can be damaged easily on the ever-present patches of gorse, rose hip and matagouri.

Perfect clothing for back-country stalking.

Flora and Fauna

Take some time out from fishing to enjoy the surroundings; there is plenty to see around the river flats and hill country. Domestic stock includes cattle, sheep, deer and the odd emu (not to be confused with the long-extinct native moa). Expect to see plenty of hares and rabbits and the sinister bird killers such as stoats, ferrets and weasels. All these small furry animals are introduced pests which the Department of

Conservation and landowners spend millions of dollars each year to control.

For the budding ornithologist, the area has plenty of native and exotic species to observe, including fantails, New Zealand pigeons (kereru), little owls, the rare New Zealand falcon, Australasian harriers, paradise ducks, mallards, grey ducks, brown teals, plovers, Canadian geese, brown and California quail, and ring-necked pheasants.

BELOW: The middle sections of the Hurunui – easy walking with splendid vistas.

THINGS TO REMEMBER

DO:
- Ask landowners for permission before proceeding.
- Check the weather forecast.
- Take insect repellent, sunscreen and food. There is plenty of cool thirst-quenching water to drink in the river.
- Wear dull clothing as the water is crystal clear and larger specimens are easily frightened, especially as the season progresses.
- Take a good selection of fly sizes, weights and patterns (sizes 10 to 16).
- Take a four-wheel-drive vehicle if proceeding beyond Lake Taylor.

DON'T:
- Leave gates open or interfere with livestock. This will eventually lead to having access denied for all future anglers.
- Expect to fish next to your car in the upper reaches.
- Leave rubbish, food scraps or discarded monofilament.
- Attempt river crossings in high water flows or if you are inexperienced.

THINGS TO DO
If your casting arm is cramping up or the weather turns nasty there's a wide array of interesting sites and exciting activities in and around the area to entertain even the most energetic traveller.
- Action and Adventure: Rafting and kayaking, jetboating, bungy jumping, mountain biking, helicopter flights, skiing, climbing, orienteering, hiking, maze, quad bikes, horse trekking, hunting.
- Eco and Nature: Guided tramping, eco-tours, whale and dolphin watching, farm visits, bird watching.
- Health and Relaxation: Spas, massage, thermal pools, walks, golf.
- Arts and Gardens: Art galleries, jewellery and crafts, rural arts.
- Food and Wine: Vineyards, wine tasting, cafés, restaurants, wine tours.
- Shows and Events: Agricultural and Pastoral Shows, wine and food celebrations, half marathons and 10 km fun runs, mountain bike races, kayak races.

Maps
For those hearty souls interested in exploring the remote upper river systems of the Hurunui we recommend the Topographical Map 260-L32 (Lake Sumner).

Resources
Christchurch i-Site Visitor Centre
(Information and Bookings)
Old Chief Post Office
Cathedral Square
Christchurch
Ph: +64-3-379 9629
Fax: +64-3-377 2424
Email: info@christchurchnz.net
info@christchurchnz.net

Hurunui Visitor Information Centre
42 Amuri Avenue
Hanmer Springs
Freephone: 0800 442 663
Ph: +64-3-315 7128
Fax: +64-3-315 7658
Email: info@hurunui.com
Web: www.hurunui.com

Hurunui Tourism
PO Box 13
Amberley
Phone: +64-3-314 8816
Fax: +64-3-314 9181

Department of Conservation
Canterbury Conservancy
133 Victoria Street
Christchurch
Ph: +64-3-379 9758
Fax: +64-3-365 1388
Email: canterburyco@doc.govt.nz

Complete Angler Fishing Store
Cnr Cashel & Barbadoes Streets
Christchurch
Ph: +64-3-366 9885
Email: complete.angler@clear.net.nz

Maui Campervans – Christchurch
530–544 Memorial Avenue
Christchurch
Ph: +64-3-358 4159
Email: nzinfo@maui-rentals.com
Web: www.maui-rentals.com

The wild and mysterious West Coast of the South Island.

"There is only one theory about angling in which I have perfect confidence, and this is that the two words least appropriate to any statement about it are the words "always" and "never"."

Lord Edward Grey (Grey of Fallodon)

ARNOLD AND GREY RIVERS

8

THE MAORI NAME FOR THE GREY RIVER IS MAWHERA MAWHERA – WIDESPREAD RIVER MOUTH. THE ARNOLD'S MAORI NAME, KOTUKUWHAKAOKA, TRANSLATES TO THE KOTUKU OR WHITE HERON, AND WHAKAOKA – TO STAB. THE KOTUKU DARTS ITS LONG, SHARP BEAK DOWN TO CATCH FISH.

The Arnold and Grey Rivers are two classic West Coast gems that drain the bush-clad, rain-swept western slopes of the Southern Alps between Reefton in the north and Lake Brunner in the south. Both rivers have separate origins but intersect near the coast where the Arnold joins the lower Grey near Stillwater, creating a single combined mass of water that surges into the Tasman Ocean at Greymouth. These river systems provide a magnificent trout habitat, continually replenished with heavy rainfall from the prevailing south-westerly weather patterns that force moisture-laden clouds formed over the Tasman Sea into the steep bush-clad slopes of the Main Divide. The dense native bush, swirling mist, and lush pasturelands make a stark contrast with the open grandeur of the east coast, and anglers lucky enough to visit are treated to wild and rugged West Coast scenery at its best.

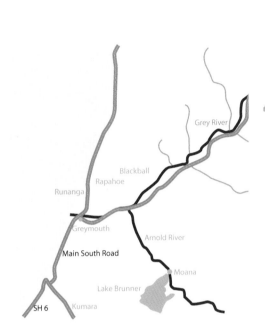

Arnold River

The Arnold is one of the region's premier rivers, a medium-sized tannin-stained waterway that drains Lake Brunner at Moana, with a deserved reputation as an excellent fly-fishing river. This is a prolific fishery for brown trout with a very stable rocky riverbed that supports a flourishing subaquatic plant ecosystem and consequently abundant insect life, which in turn feeds a large healthy trout population. Regular drift-dive surveys indicate a brown trout population as high as 240 fish per kilometre.

There are 24 km (15 miles) of fishable water from the lake to the confluence with the Grey, which remains fishable even after heavy rain, with Lake Brunner acting as a filter, preventing undue discolouration. The river is slow and serene in the upper sections. Banks are overgrown with trees and scrub, flax and reeds, and fishing from shore is difficult, with limited access. These upper reaches are best fished by boat and local guides often use North American-style drift boats.

Midway down the river, downstream of Kotuku, there is a small hydroelectric power station and a small lake section with some excellent lagoons and shallows where fish may be spotted cruising for insects and minnows. The middle to lower sections from Kotuku through to Stillwater run parallel to the Arnold Valley Road and offer exceptional nymph and dry-fly fishing for which the river has become deservedly famous. Two small tributaries, Molloy Creek and Deep Creek, flow through farmland into the Arnold near Kotuku and are both worth investigating.

Grey River

The Grey River forms the main artery in a large system with several tributaries and lakes that

Grizzly Emerger – one of the lethal traditional British 'wee wet patterns', just as effective on New Zealand rivers. Fish in the evening with another traditional wet or nymph.

OPPOSITE: Malcolm Bell dwarfed by the magnificent West Coast bush.

ABOVE: Prime water on the Arnold just waiting for a fly.

ABOVE RIGHT: The Arnold River vegetation can be hard to penetrate. Kent takes a short cut along the route of the famous TranzAlpine.

drain the expansive catchment on the western slopes of the Southern Alps from Reefton in the north to Lake Poerua in the south. The river offers a huge variety of fishable water with a large head of brown trout and boasting one of the highest catch rates on the West Coast. It would take weeks to do justice to all the angling opportunities available in the Grey watershed, including the spring and rain-fed lakes such as Lakes Brunner, Poerua, Haupiri, Hochstetter and Lady Lake. This is without mentioning the many tributaries, some of which are outstanding fisheries in their own right, such as the Rough River (Otututu), which joins the Grey River near Ikamatua.

Adventurous anglers can select a character that suits from the huge range of different fishing water as the river changes character dramatically on its long journey through the valley. There's endless opportunity to chase a seemingly inexhaustible supply of brown trout.

Water clarity varies throughout the river system, ranging from tea or tannin coloured or sediment discoloured to crystal clear. Anglers have the opportunity to sight fish or prospect by blind casting where visibility is restricted. During spring and early summer anglers also have the opportunity to target sea-run brown trout and the occasional salmon, especially in the lower reaches. Spin and bait fishing are popular in the lower Grey River and many other West Coast rivers and estuaries but the avid fly angler can do very well when large shoals of sea runs enter the river to gorge themselves on the revered West Coast whitebait and other baitfish. There is even the opportunity to catch these beautiful specimens when walking the banks of the river around the mouth at Greymouth township by casting to feeding fish with whitebait or bully-imitation streamer flies.

Getting There

The West Coast has no international airports but there are domestic airline or charter flights to Hokitika Airport; it is only a half hour's drive from the airport to the fisheries in the Grey River catchment. The majority of visiting anglers arrive by road from the east coast via Arthur's Pass on State Highway 73. The drive alone is worth doing just for the magnificent scenery and

- Below the Arnold Dam (salmon, December to March).
- Kokiri Bridge by the freezing works.
- Old Arnold Road between the Arnold River and Arnold Valley Road
- Upstream of Arnold Creek (signposted).
- Aratika, which is sign posted on the gate. Contact R.L. or D.M. Milne on phone +64-3-738 0038.
- Arnold River Bridge near Aratika.
- Kotoku: take the road following the true right of Molloy Creek.
- Moana Footbridge at the outlet of Lake Brunner.

LEFT: You will see some impressive road engineering travelling through Arthur's Pass.

there are numerous interesting attractions and many excellent trout waters to explore between Christchurch and Greymouth.

Allow four hours for the drive, or for a more romantic, relaxed journey board the famous TranzAlpine express. This is one of New Zealand's most impressive and scenic rail journeys. The trip departs daily, is 223.8 km (139 miles) long and takes just four and a half hours. There are 16 tunnels and five viaducts, the highest in the Staircase standing at 73 m (240 ft.).

Alternative road routes to Greymouth that are all worthy of note for their touring qualities are along State Highway 6 from the south through the Haast Pass, which runs through the beautiful Mt Aspiring National Park. From Westport in the north, along the coastal route past the famous Punakaiki Pancake Rocks or via the inland route on State Highway 7 from Reefton through the old gold-mining fields.

Access
Arnold River
The Arnold joins the Grey River 15 km (9.3 miles) from Greymouth at Stillwater and there are a number of access points, although anglers should choose carefully to avoid battling the heavy barrier of undergrowth along much of the riverbank. Anglers unfamiliar with the area can avoid misadventure by using the marked access points along Arnold Valley Rd:

LEFT AND BELOW: A typical Grey River brown trout before and after.

Spin fishing for the delicious sea-run browns (far right) at one of the many West Coast river mouths.

Grey River

There is easy access to the middle and lower river with roads running along both banks up to Ikamatua. Commonly used access points include Greymouth, Omoto Racecourse, Taylorville, Stillwater Bridge, Matai, Blackball, Ahaura, Totara Flat and Ikamatua. Where the river does not run alongside the road, permission must be obtained from landowners to cross their land. Please respect property, fasten gates and leave no litter.

There are many kilometres of excellent fishing in the upper reaches of the Grey and the section below the confluence of the Brown and Blue Grey rivers is popular with local anglers. Fish average around 2 kg (4.4 lb.) in this section and the water is usually crystal clear, allowing anglers to stalk and sight fish their quarry. There is limited road

access to the upper river via Palmer Road, Golf Links Road and Waipuna Road, which all run off State Highway 7. The river runs through private farmland, often some distance from the road. Always get the landowner's permission before crossing farms.

Angling

The Grey River system is an extremely productive wild brown-trout fishery with both resident and visiting sea runs. An additional bonus is the quinnat salmon run which usually occurs between late December to March. The section of the Grey between Omoto and Ahaura is a popular area to target salmon, but the runs vary considerably from year to year and most are caught by spin fishers pursuing trout.

The sea-run browns are astonishingly beautiful, being more silvery and streamlined than their resident cousins. They are very impressive and acrobatic fighters and superb eating with firm red flesh similar in colour to wild salmon. The average sea run that can be expected is around 1 to 1.5 kg (2.2 to 3.3 lb.) but fish to 4 kg (8.8 lb.) are caught every season. Resident browns in the Arnold and lower and middle Grey River average 1 to 2 kg (2.2 to 4.4 lb.), often in high concentrations of between 200 to 250 fish per kilometre. The upper Grey and tributaries generally have lower stocks but anglers prepared to walk will encounter trophy fish to 4 kg (8.8 lb.).

Season

Arnold River: Open all year. Bag limit of four fish.
Grey: The fishery is divided into two sections:
- Upper reaches – above the Clarke River confluence, 1 October to 30 April.
- Middle and lower reaches – above the Clarke River confluence, open all year.
Bag limit is four fish although catch and release is encouraged in the upper river.

Techniques and Tactics

Most fly anglers concentrate their efforts on dry-fly and nymph fishing to sighted fish or blind fishing in the deeper or discoloured water. The Arnold River is especially popular with dry-fly enthusiasts during the prolific evening hatches of October–November and March–April. However, the magnitude and variety of fishable water in the

Grey catchment offers fantastic opportunities to experiment and use alternative styles of fishing in a wide range of water and terrains. All methods of presenting a fly including dry, nymphing, traditional wet flies or large streamers can be highly successful when applied correctly. There is great scope to explore new methods and play with different lines and flies. This is a great location to try drift boat fishing, with the Grey alone having over 80 km (50 miles) of water to cover. A local guide is a very wise investment with several offering both still-water and river-boating options.

With high trout densities, anglers do not necessarily have to walk far and it is common for competent anglers to take several fish from the

Fly-rodding sea-run browns in an estuary is a unique challenge.

same pool or run. A willingness to try a range of techniques and making changes to match the conditions will pay dividends and allow you to take fish throughout the day. If there has been heavy rain in the region, head for the Arnold, which usually remains fishable. The Grey can become swollen and dirty and has a reputation for rising very quickly so take special care if there has been a lot of rain. Even in the heaviest of rainstorms anglers can head to Lake Brunner or one of the smaller lakes in the watershed.

As well as a floating line, carry a medium sinker or sinking shooting head, or alternatively some sinking extensions to add to your floating line. We usually keep to single lengths of 3.5 kg (8 lb.) fluorocarbon for leaders, although you may need to reduce this to 2.7 kg (6 lb.) if fishing the gin-clear waters of the upper Grey.

The Arnold is permanently stained with tree tannin resembling a brew of dark tea, which

FAR RIGHT: Try using flashy smelt imitations on sea-run browns.

makes sight fishing very difficult. In the absence of rising fish, the best strategy is to probe likely holding water with a double nymph rig with a small yarn indicator or a dry fly with a nymph dropper suspended beneath during daylight. Both rigs are also effective on the Grey, although fish can more often be spotted especially in the clear upper sections and tributaries.

Rods rated for lines between #5 and #7 weight are a good choice, enabling reasonable casting distance but maintaining enough delicacy to

A pristine Arnold brown.

present flies naturally to feeding fish. Keep leaders reasonably short, somewhere between 2.4 and 3.3 m (8 and 11 ft.) will suffice, which helps when back casts become restricted by the dense vegetation. It is useful to have a basic roll cast in your repertoire to reach some pockets.

Use reasonably small size-14 or 16 nymphs with a little lead or tungsten weight as these rivers flow deceptively swiftly. In the warmer months you are likely to experience significant hatches of caddis or mayfly, often in the evening, although it is not unusual to have several fish dimpling a stretch of water at any time of the day. Match the hatch and don't hesitate to switch flies if the fish ignore your first offering. Try two dry patterns of various sizes or a dry and emerger or Spent Spinner combination. It pays to be observant and watch insect life to determine the type, colour and size for guidance on pattern selection. If fish continue to ignore upstream dries and emergers, try switching to a tandem rig of 'wee traditional wet flies' and swing these subsurface across and downstream on a floating or slow-sinking line. This has proved a lethal approach on many rivers, especially in the evening rise when fish are refusing dries, and it works equally effectively when blind fishing the shallow and tails of pools.

For real excitement, try fishing small wets into the dark; the strikes are often savage grabs as fish have less time to inspect imitations and tend to lose their daytime shyness after sunset. Be warned that darkness is the hunting time for monster browns and your gear needs to be able to handle hard deep runs, so make sure you have plenty of backing!

An amazing resource often overlooked by fly anglers are the hard-fighting sea-run browns that provide a unique sport-fishing option and can be found in large numbers in many of the West Coast estuaries and lower rivers. The sight of packs of silvery trout crashing through panicked whitebait on the surface is enough to mesmerise any angler. Even better, these fish are far from shy in hunting mode and will demolish a whitebait

Precariously balanced for the cast.

imitation stripped at high speed on floating or sinking lines. We had a memorable evening session spinning and fly fishing in the surf at the mouth of the Okuru River. We had spotted schools of the hard-fighting sea fish kahawai hunting anchovies and whitebait but we started catching beautiful speckled sea-run brownies as well as kahawai. Don't be put off if fish are not active; try strolling the banks and cast and retrieve near any schools of baitfish. The lower rivers, including the estuarine section in the centre of Greymouth, are good places to search for sea-run trout. During the middle of the day try using a high-density shooting headline. Swing white, grey or silver smelt patterns through the depths by casting across river and using a short jerky retrieve. Heavier rods in the #8 to #9 weight range make casting large streamer wet flies easier and provide greater distance to cover the deep, wide sections of river.

Flies and Rigs

It pays to carry a good selection of flies in various sizes. This is a location where dries, nymphs, emergers, traditional wet flies and streamers are

Sea-run heaven!

all effective. However, as in any form of fishing, a great starting point is to match the food type and try to present your artificial as naturally as possible. Useful nymph patterns include Hare's Ear, Halfback and caddis larvae imitations. Don't be afraid to use a small fluffy indicator to help detect strikes, especially in the faster broken water. A good base starter kit of dry flies is Royal Wulff, Adams, Blue Dun, Greenwell's Glory and Kakahi Queen but any mayfly or caddis imitations will take fish so don't be afraid to experiment. Don't leave home without a selection of simple traditional wet flies; these should be small – sizes 10, 12 and 14, with thin, sparsely dressed bodies.

Try patterns like March Brown and Mallard and Claret or the wet-fly version of the Blue Dun or Greenwell's Glory. If you had to select one pattern for the Grey catchment, the classic mayfly imitation the Blue Dun, dressed as either a wet or dry fly, would be our first choice.

If you are lucky enough to be around during the sea-run trout runs, any good smelt imitation will work. One of the oldest and most popular New Zealand wet flies, Parsons Glory, can be a real killer as can the Grey Ghost, Rabbit-style and Matuku-style streamers or perhaps use overseas favourites like Pearl Flashabou or Dog Nobblers in white or grey.

Tips and Tricks

Fish your feet first in these waters. Brown trout have a habit of hugging the banks, patrolling back eddies and sitting tight in the riffles and the neutral water just to the side of the turbulent white water at the head of rapids at the top of pools and runs. During the day focus on pockets of water with neutral zones adjacent to faster-flowing currents and feed lanes. Classic lies include behind or just ahead of large rocks, boulders or logs, against banks and under overhanging vegetation or directly under secondary rapids away from the main flow.

Brown trout often tend to inhabit shallower water and different lies to rainbows. Don't waste too much time and energy fishing the middle of deeper pools or runs with little obvious structure. If there is no obvious insect-based feeding or fish herding baitfish, concentrate towards the head and sides of reaches. Where water clarity allows, scan carefully with Polaroids for a telltale shadow or gently swaying tail. These browns are perfectly camouflaged for this environment and you need to move slowly and false cast carefully to avoid disturbing your quarry.

While the selection of a fly that matches available food is important, the critical key to regular success is the selection of leader length and having the correctly weighted nymph. The fish in these rivers are well fed and generally will not move far to intercept your offering. Our favourite exploratory rig is a nymph suspended under a dry fly, but we will constantly change the length of the dropper and weight of the nymph to match the speed and depth of water. When covering shallow riffles the dropper may be only a few inches long but with a medium-weighted nymph to gain depth quickly. Conversely, a long glide or slower-moving water might suit a long dropper of a metre (39 in.) or more but with a lightly weighted nymph that drifts down naturally in the current.

With fish that have been spotted, stop to think about your rig before casting and take the extra time to adapt your leader system and fly to reach the required depth. Always treat your dry flies regularly to ensure they float well and have sufficient buoyancy to suspend a point fly if you are using a tandem rig.

With a one or two-nymph rig on the Arnold River or other discoloured water, it is worthwhile using a small indicator to help detect takes. Providing this is kept reasonably small and naturally coloured it should not alert fish. Try a small white fluff or wool indicator, as there is usually plenty of white foam thrown out of the fast water and drifting down current lines to make a white strike indicator innocuous.

Equipment and Apparel

Put a high-quality insect repellent at the top of your list if you want to return with your sanity intact. The West Coast may be beautiful but a few minutes unprotected from the constant attacks from sandflies and mosquitoes will dim your views on the scenic splendours and incredible fishing. Use repellent with a good percentage of DEET (N,N-diethyl-meta-toluamide). Some brands combine an effective UV-resistant sunscreen – another essential in summer. As a general rule it tends to be sandflies by day and mosquitoes

Expect to catch quite a few hard-fighting kahawai when targeting sea-run browns.

The West Coast is an ornithologist's utopia; keas (above) and wekas (below right) are known for their inquisitive natures.

requirement for deep wading, but in situations where anglers are considering crossing or chasing runaway fish they should be particularly cautious.

Flora and Fauna

The forests of the West Coast are denser and more lush than those of the east coast and are enveloped in a seemingly continuous cloud of moisture in the form of rain, drizzle and mist. The terrain is wild, broken and rugged; black sand beaches loaded with endless piles of driftwood give way to river flats, foothills and near vertical slopes draped in dense swathes of native podocarp forest including giants like rimu, matai, totara, miro and rata. The slopes are dissected by serpentine streams and cascading waterfalls and are often shrouded in dense blankets of cloud and thick steam rising from the forests. Rising sharply in the background and covered with glistening snow are the towering majestic mountain faces and summits of the Southern Alps.

On the lowlands and river flats there are rare stands of kahikatea forest bordering lakes and wetlands. Ferns and mosses abound in the damp environment and the farm pastures and thickets of bush are dotted with sedges, rushes, red tussock and flax and raupo swamps.

All the common native birds are still present in high numbers in this part of Westland, including kea, kaka, weka and brown kiwis. This is also one of the last havens for several rare and endangered species including the Fiordland crested penguin, yellowhead, blue ducks (whio) and the great spotted kiwi, and one species of native bat.

at night. If you intend to tramp and camp, take a tent with a sealed insect screen inner. The mosquitoes do not carry any parasites such as malaria but they will succeed in driving you mad if you are not protected. Keep insect repellent and sunscreen away from fly lines, sunglasses, camera lenses and plastics to avoid corrosive damage. We also carry lightweight gloves and always wear long-sleeved collared shirts to cover as much skin as possible.

Most Kiwi anglers tend to opt for tramping boots, polypropylene leggings and quick-drying shorts. This ensemble is not for the fashion conscious but is very effective in keeping you warm in the cold, as well as being cool and breathable in summer and safe from insects and the numerous thorny plants.

Lightweight breathable waders or thigh waders are also a good choice, although you can overheat if intending on walking a long way. You also need to be careful not to puncture them on the vegetation. As with all waders, a waist belt should be worn to prevent the leggings filling with water if you have a fall. Much of the Grey catchment can be fished dry from the banks or by shallow wading to knee level. There is little

Whitebait, a tiny translucent fish, are prolific and receive a great deal of focus given their importance both culturally and economically to Westland. Southern fur seals spend their winters near Knights Point, Galway Beach and Jacksons Bay. Many of the introduced land mammals have thrived in the wild and are classified as pests and subject to frequent control and eradication programmes. Red deer, goats, possums, stoats and weasels are found in lowland and montane forests. Above the bushline there are chamois and Himalayan thar, both sought-after prizes for hunters.

THINGS TO REMEMBER

DO:

- Ask at the local sports stores regarding where to fish and always get landowners' permission before crossing private land.
- Check the weather forecast, recent rainfall and river conditions.
- Take insect repellent, sunscreen, food and a torch (flashlight).
- Expect to get rained upon. Pack quality wet-weather gear and a change of clothes.
- Take a good selection of patterns, sizes, weights and styles of flies (sizes 10 to 16).
- Tell someone where you are going and your expected time of return. This is a big, sparsely populated watershed and it is particularly remote in the upper eaches.

DON'T:

- Attempt night fishing unless you have familiarised yourself with the location in daylight.
- Camp or leave vehicles in riverbeds or run-off areas. The Grey catchment is subject to flash flooding and rivers swell quickly and dangerously.
- Attempt river crossings in high water flows or if you are inexperienced.
- Try taking short cuts to the riverbanks through thick bush. The West Coast vegetation can be virtually impenetrable and unforgiving. Keep to paths and follow local advice on access.
- Feel you have to walk far to catch fish. These are high-population rivers in the middle and lower reaches and good numbers of fish can be hooked without covering much distance. Many spots with excellent fishing prospects can be reached within sight of your vehicle.

THINGS TO DO

Greymouth is now one of the largest tourist destinations on the West Coast with an interesting array of spectacular and interesting attractions.

- Action and Adventure: Caving and canyoning, kayaking, canoeing, four-wheel-drive off-road rallying, climbing and abseiling, quad biking and motorbiking, rafting, hunting and shooting, deep-sea fishing, tramping, camping.
- Eco and Nature: Fox and Franz Joseph Glaciers tours, natural wildlife tours, Punakaiki scenic landscape, guided walks, scenic flights.
- Health and Relaxation: History museums, tourist shopping and souvenirs.
- Arts and Gardens: Arts and crafts, greenstone (New Zealand jade).
- Food and Wine: Cafés, restaurants.
- Shows and Events: Hokitika Wildfoods Festival.

Maps
Topographical Maps 260-J31 (Greymouth), 260-K31 (Ahaura), 260-K32 (Lake Brunner).

Resources
Greymouth i-SITE Visitor Centre
Cnr Mackay and Herbert Streets
Greymouth
Free phone: 0800 473 966
Ph: +64-3-768 5101
Fax: +64-3-768 0317
Email: vingm@minidata.co.nz
Web: www.westcoastbookings.co.nz

Department of Conservation
Greymouth Mawheranui Area Office
23 High Street
Greymouth
Ph: +64-3-768 0427
Fax: +64-3-768 7417

www.tranzscenic.co.nz
www.tourism.net.nz/region/west-coast/
www.greymouth-tourism.nzld.com

Another South Island rainbow falls to the dry fly.

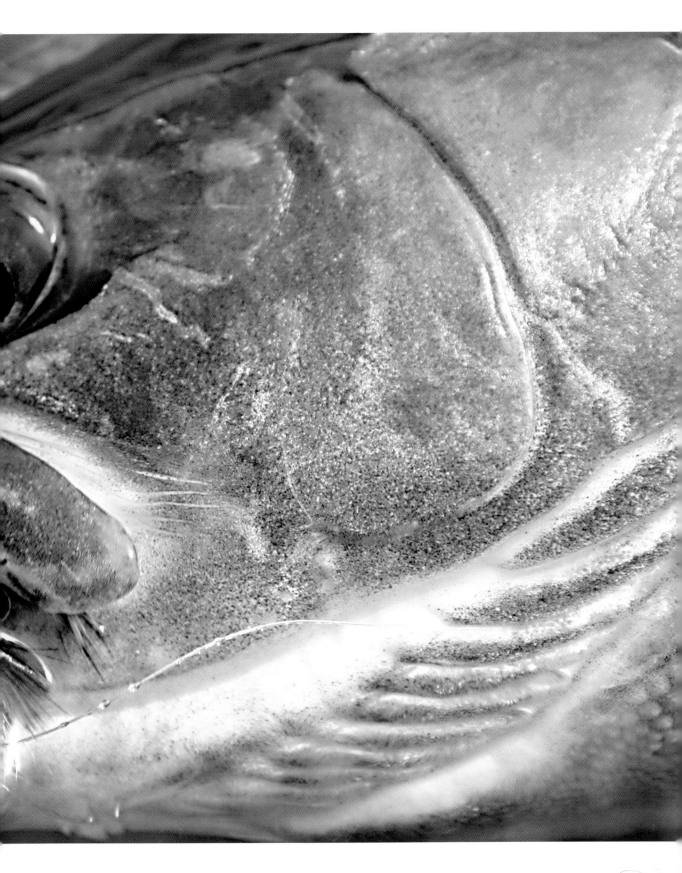

'Even eminent chartered accountants are known, in their capacity as fishermen, blissfully to ignore differences between seven and ten inches, half a pound and two pounds, three fish and a dozen fish.'

William Sherwood Fox, *Silken Lines and Silver Hooks*

RANGITATA RIVER

9

RANGI (SKY OR DAY); TATA (LOWERING CLOUDS) — PERHAPS NAMED ON ONE OF THOSE DAYS WHEN CLOUD COVER FLOWS LOW OVER THE ALPS INTO THE RANGITATA BASIN.

The Rangitata River epitomises the South Island's braided rivers. It winds its way down the valley towards the Pacific Ocean in a pattern determined by the forces of nature and set in such a vast expanse of stunning vistas that it can leave you neglecting to notice the less grand, yet equally beautiful, scenes like the colours of the matagouri berry or squadrons of Canada geese flying overhead. This is one of the areas made famous by *The Lord of the Rings* feature film that brought New Zealand to the rest of the world.

Although unspoilt, the Rangitata is ever changing because of the very nature of braided rivers. Last year's hot spot may be a dry piece of bank in the new season after snow and flood has restructured the river. In fact, it can be like fishing a whole maze of little rivers. To achieve results in this river you must be prepared to walk and wade and look for the telltale signs of areas that will hold fish. For example, water cascading down from one braid into a larger braid creates a well-oxygenated area with a constant supply of food. Other spots to look for are where the river winds towards more solid banks lined with vegetation, or deeper runs that offer cover and currents that create lanes along which food will be carried. You need to keep an eye for simple things like the direction of the wind that will blow terrestrial life onto the water.

The Rangitata River is famous as one of the major salmon rivers in the South Island and also boasts good populations of rainbow and brown trout. The brown trout are both resident and sea run. The angling options start at the mouth right through to the headwaters and include a few spring creeks that can offer excellent prospects. Picking a time to fish the Rangitata can be tricky

as snow melt and rainfall can turn the river milky and make it impossible to spot fish. The volume of the river, measured in cubic metres per second (cumecs), determines the swiftness of the current and depth of crossings areas. Too high a flow and access to fishing can be very limited. The ideal levels are around 80 cumecs.

Getting There

Allow two and a half hours to travel to the upper reaches of the Rangitata from Christchurch. The roads are good most of the way but you travel on gravel roads for the last part of the journey. A good road map will get you there without incident.

Rangitata Mouth

There are fishing hut settlements on both north and south sides of the river mouth. To reach the north side, travel via the Hinds-Rangitata Mouth Road, which turns off from State Highway 1 towards the coast, 2 km (1.2 miles) south of Hinds township. For the south side, turn off State Highway 1 and follow the signpost directions.

Caddilac Pheasant Tail – a very good prospecting nymph for fast water. Weight with a tungsten bead and bounce along the bottom.

OPPOSITE: A spectacular view up the Rangitata river.

Firing a dry fly into likely-looking water in a side braid.

North Bank – North Side Huts to State Highway 1

Between the north side huts and State Highway 1 there are two main access points from Coldstream Road at the irrigation outfall (8.5 km or 5 miles) and Old Main South Road (16 km or 9.9 miles).

South Bank – Mouth to Mesopotamia

On the south side, access to the river is available at Badham Road (known as Wades Crossing).

Proceeding upstream via Arundel-Rangitata Road, the river can be accessed at Lewis Road (6 km or 3.7 miles from State Highway 1) before joining Regional Route 72 at the Arundel Bridge (10 km or 6.2 miles). Best parking at Arundel Bridge is on the south side.

From Arundel Bridge, travel via Ferry Road to Peel Forest and then along Rangitata Gorge Road. Access to the river is at Ferry Road, Peel Forest camping ground, Lynn Stream, Mt Peel Station and Raules Gully.

At this point the road swings away from the river but rejoins it at Whiterock Station. At Rata Peaks, 10 km (6.2 miles) upstream from here, Fisherman's Lane leads to the river. Access is also available at Forest Creek, a further 8 km (4.9 miles) towards Mesopotamia.

North Bank – Arundel to Klondyke

There is only one access point in this section. From Arundel Bridge continue along Regional Route 72 for 6 km (3.7 miles) and turn off at the

Five Crossroads corner along Ealing-Montalto Road. This is a public road only as far as the Rangitata Diversion Race (RDR) bridge (2 km or 1.2 miles). Beyond there for the next 4 km (2.4 miles) to the river the road is owned and maintained by RDR Management Ltd who allow vehicle access at your own risk.

The road ends at the RDR intake; beyond there the landowners of Klondike and Tenehaun Stations permit foot access only to allow anglers to fish the gorge area.

Angling

The Rangitata River is famous for both its trout angling and salmon fishery. It originates high in the Southern Alps and is prone to floods and freshes from high rainfall and snowmelt, particularly during warm north-west wind conditions that occur frequently throughout the main salmon season from November to March. However, the duration of unfishable periods is usually short and good fishing can be experienced as discoloured waters begin to clear. The best fishing at the mouth is generally December and January. Upriver salmon fishing is better from January to March. The Rangitata is also noted for its sea-run brown trout early in the season.

Season

The Rangitata is open below the State Highway No.1 Bridge for the summer season from 1 October to 30 April and the main river excluding tributaries has a winter season from 1 June to 31 August. Above the State Highway 1 Bridge to Turn Again Point (shown by the white posts on the riverbank about 15km above the gorge) the river and its tributaries are open for the summer season from 1 October to 30 April.

Above Turn Again Point, the river and tributaries are open for fishing from 1 October with the season for salmon running to the last day of February and the season for trout running to 31 March.

The Rangitata diversion race from the intake downstream to Rakaia River Road is open all year.

The daily bag limit downstream from Turn Again Point is six sports fish of which no more than two may be salmon and no more than four may be trout. Above Turn Again Point the daily bag limit is four sports fish of which no more than two may be salmon and no more than two may be trout. In the winter season (below SH1 Bridge) the limit is two sports fish. The minimum length for salmon killed is 30 cm.

Techniques and Tactics

Be prepared for a good walk when you fish the Rangitata River. The likely places to fish are where the braids head towards a solid bank or some vegetation beside the river. Cover the water quickly so as to not waste time on the unproductive zones. When you find some fish holding water, take more time and cover the water more thoroughly. Look for structure, even obstacles in the river bed like logs provide a potential haunt for finding fish. Pay special attention to main braids that carry more water volume and particularly when these swing against a bank or form a hole or pool. More often than not you will see the telltale sign of salmon anglers foot prints around these holes and deeper depressions.

Malcolm Bell hangs on as a hefty rainbow takes off downstream.

Flies and Rigs

Although shallow, the Rangitata River moves along at a fair pace and a pair of small dark tungsten bead-head nymphs on a long leader is a good set-up to use when prospecting. Add a piece of float dough about half the size of a pea as an indicator half way up your leader. When the conditions are right, fish in the Rangitata will rise freely to dry flies even if there is no obvious hatch at the time. This may be because of the stark environment or that the fish are feeding on windswept terrestrials. Dries that imitate blow flies do work especially well, one of the favourites being a size 12 to 14 dark Royal Wulff-type pattern tied with a Peacock body. These work best fished along edges of the banks and where braids connect. A dry fly with a lightly-weighted nymph suspended a metre below is a good exploratory rig. Try a large Coch-y-Bondhu with a small Hare and Copper nymph in sizes 12 to 16 underneath.

Tips and Tricks

The wind direction and angle of the sun are very important when fishing the Rangitata River as the terrain offers very little elevation for spotting fish and you really have to look for windows to spot into. Obviously, with strong winds or overcast days it can be near impossible to spot fish. Take these factors into account when fishing this region. The Rangitata is one river that rewards the early starter, as the fish are less likely to have been disturbed and the wind usually picks up during the day. Much of the water will be devoid of fish. Keep thinking about structure and where food is likely to concentrate. Cast as you walk and keep moving until you are either spotting or getting takes from your quarry.

Equipment and Apparel

A day's fishing on the Rangitata River could see you easily covering 6–10 kms of fishable water so it pays to carry extra gear in a good comfortable day pack, hiking through rivers and uneven terrain can drain energy reserves quickly. Carrying a couple of high energy protein bars or muesli bars and an energy drink in your fly vest can provide a much needed boost if reserves get too low.

Walking the boulder strewn braided Rangitata River can be hard on equipment and body alike. Good quality boots will go a long way to preventing rolled ankles and blistered feet. The walk back to the car always seems to be the longest after a day on the river. Dress to account for the changeable nature of the weather in this area. Always carry warm lightweight clothing and rainwear that also works as a windbreaker, even if you don't have to use it. Skies are often very clear and the light very intense, unprotected heads and eyes are easily burned. Large broad brim hats with a chin strap, matched with

LEFT: A floating line with plenty of backing is all the equipment you need to take when fishing the Rangitata.

FAR LEFT: A small, weighty tungsten bead-head nymph deceived this healthy brown trout.

polarised glasses covering the eye fully, offer the necessary protection and aid immensely with fish spotting. Due to the drying nature of the often cool environment sun protection can easily be overlooked. Carry a good quality sunblock and apply every half an hour, use a separate chapstick on lips, ears and nose for extra protection.

Two little pieces of equipment that prove their worth time after time is a small torch that can light a track, or signal a companion, and a small pocket knife or multi tool that seriously will get put to uses you would have never considered — like the time we had to rescue a bull that was entangled in a wire fence. The multi tool was used to cut the wires and save the animal, which was clearly in distress, and would have died if not for the cutters.

Flora and Fauna

The Rangitata River provides habitat for a wide variety of native bird species, including blue duck (whio). The river also provides habitat for good populations of mallard ducks and Canada geese. During the roar the period when deer are mating, it is not uncommon to hear wild deer that make their home in the hills.

The rugged terrain is mainly covered in Mataguori and grasses which seem devoid of much in the way of plant life. On closer inspection

Keep alert, ready for the take.

the area is rich in a wide variety of flora. Some of this is very unique and have botanists running off all kinds of Latin descriptions.

Glacial scouring of the land has left a unique map of events through the ages. Fossils and semiprecious stones give a look back into the early days of this region and offer a true insight into how the region has formed.

THINGS TO REMEMBER

DO:

- Allow plenty of time to walk the river.
- Leave the environment undisturbed.
- Keep an eye out for the upper fishing limit markers.
- Check the river levels.
- Watch for changes in the weather.

DON'T

- Enter the river above another angler.
- Cross the river in swift or deep areas.
- Cross the river after dark.
- Overlook back waters for fishing.
- Cast shadows on the water.
- Disturb spawning salmon.

THINGS TO DO

South Canterbury is largely a farming district. Ashburton, Timaru and Temuka offer all the facilities a traveller could need in smaller semi-rural settings. Activities around the region are numerous and the river is widely used for other recreational activities. A good way to truly appreciate this region is to stay in a farm stay which are generally very comfortable and provide a good insight into the farming lifestyle not to mention very hearty meals.

- Action and Adventure: Rafting and kayaking, jet boating, mountain biking, helicopter flights, hiking, hot-air ballooning, sky diving, hunting, skiing
- Eco and Nature: Guided tramping, eco-tours, farm visits, bird watching, nature photography, 4x4 tours, fossil hunting.
- Health and Relaxation: walks, golf.
- Arts and Gardens: art galleries, jewelry and crafts, rural arts.
- Food and Wine: vineyards, wine tasting, cafés, restaurants, village pubs.

Maps

For the main back-country portion of the Rangitata River use Topographical Map 260-J36 (Mt Harper/Mahaanui). The lower and middle sections can easily be found on a good road map.

Resources

Ashburton i-Site Visitor Centre
East Street
Ashburton
Ph: +64-3-308 1050
Fax: +64-3-308 1064
Email: ashburton@i-site.org
Web: www.ashburtontourism.co.nz

Department of Conservation
Canterbury Conservancy
133 Victoria Street
Christchurch
Ph: +64-3-379 9758
Fax: +64-3-365 1388
Email: canterburyco@doc.govt.nz

Complete Angler Fishing Store
Cnr Cashel and Barbadoes Streets
Christchurch
Ph: +64-3-366 9885
Email: complete.angler@clear.net.nz

Maui Campervans – Christchurch
530–544 Memorial Avenue
Christchurch
Ph: +64-3-358 4159
Email: nzinfo@maui-rentals.com
Web: www.maui-rentals.com

www.fishandgame.org.nz

Searching for trout
on the main braid.

Lake Benmore at dawn.

'The charm of fishing is that it is the pursuit of what is elusive but attainable, a perpetual series of occasions for hope.'

– John Buchan

AHURIRI RIVER

10

DERIVED FROM TU AHURIRI. THE MISSIONARY WILLIAM COLENSO SUGGESTED THE NAME MEANS 'FIERCE RUSHING', AN ALLUSION TO THE SWIFT FLOW.

The Ahuriri is best described as a complex river system with a diversity of water throughout its long journey from the Alps to Lake Benmore. From the sedate oxbow lagoons where the river flows into Lake Benmore up through the semi-structured branched lower reaches, in to areas of gorge strewn with boulders and then changing to the highland tussock country system that is common to many of the headwaters of South Island rivers that start their life in the Southern Alps. Despite the stark differences in terrain, the river is magnificently scenic wherever you choose to cast a line. The very nature and complexity of the Ahuriri is what makes it such a pleasure to fish. It is quite possible to explore the headwaters in the morning, stalking browns on terrestrial imitations, then target feisty rainbows on sunken nymphs in the gently flowing mid reaches and finish the day angling into dusk at the sandy mouth of the river where it enters Lake Benmore with streamer flies casually stripped just off the bottom on a slow-sinking line. The Ahuriri should be a must-visit on any angler's itinerary of rivers to fish in the South Island.

Getting There

A great place for anglers to base themselves is at the small settlement of Omarama, which offers anglers good access to all areas of the river with very short travel times. Situated near the middle of the South Island the area is a good regional base with the closest major city being Timaru in the east, which is about three hours travelling at a leisurely pace. State Highway 8 heads west from Omarama to a signpost for Ahuriri Conservation Park, which comprises over 49,000 hectares (120,000 acres) of rugged mountain country,

wetlands, tussock lands and forest. If you head east from Omarama on State Highway 83, it will lead you to the Ahuriri Arm of Lake Benmore and access to the lower river. The Upper Ahuriri Valley Road is suitable only for four-wheel-drive vehicles and is subject to frequent washouts and slips during and after periods of heavy rainfall or snow melt. Heavy snowfall in winter and thaw cycles in the late winter and early spring can make the road impassable.

Prince Nymph – American anglers use these unweighted during a buzzer rise but it has proved to be a lethal nymph in Kiwi waters either weighted or unweighted.

LEFT: The highway bridge provides good access to the middle river.

OPPOSITE: A good catch on the Ahuriri.

A healthy brown in the bag.

Access

One of the attractions of the Ahuriri is the vast amount of access to fishable water. At Lake Benmore a roughly marked track leads across a swampy area to the delta mouth area, which

Checking the information about the Ahuriri conservation area.

has excellent prospects and the lower braids of the river can be fished unimpeded upstream. A small boat can also be launched in Lake Benmore and beached at the mouth, or used to stalk fish that cruise the lagoons. Alternatively, the lower reaches can be reached by strolling downstream from the SH8 road bridge . If you are heading to the middle and upper sections in the Ahuriri Conservation Park, the river can be accessed at various marked anglers' access signs and the entire length of the river can be prospected with relatively easy river crossings. The park offers some interesting tramps to reach more isolated spots. Even though the walking is fairly easy, wear good tramping boots and pack warm apparel and take adequate provisions. Take care when walking through the tussock country as it is very easy to roll an ankle in this uneven terrain.

Angling

Rainbow and brown trout are both present in the river. Throughout the season fish will be found in different parts of the river: the upper river tends to hold the better-quality browns while the mouth and lower river have a higher concentration of rainbows averaging 1.5 to 2 kg (3.3 to 4.4 lb.). The river is productive all season with the early-season fish particularly zealous to take a fly both on the surface and subsurface after a long rest from angling pressure over the closed winter period. In the latter part of the season the fish can be difficult to locate, requiring more prospecting, as the trout move through the river for spawning and can prove more wary. The condition of the late-season fish is generally very good and worth the effort with trophy fish around 4.5 kg (10 lb.) being caught every season.

Season

The season for the upper Ahuriri River above Longslip Creek including the tributaries runs from the first Saturday in December until 30 April. The bag limit is two fish.

Below Longslip Creek the open season is 1 October– 30 April and the bag limit is four trout.

Techniques and Tactics

Having a good arsenal of techniques and the ability to respond to the changing character of the Ahuriri will reward anglers with good catches. A standard 2.75 m (9 ft.) #6 weight rod is ideal for all parts of the Ahuriri River. Carrying a natural-coloured weight-forward floating fly line and an intermediate or very slow sinker which can be very useful when the norwesterly wind makes upriver casting impossible.

Take a flexible approach and be prepared to change quickly from dry fly to a pair of weighted nymphs to cover the bottom depth or slip on a couple of subsurface wet flies if fish start to bulge on emergers or the wind becomes a nuisance. In good conditions you can sight fish. Having a buddy to do the spotting from a vantage point

where they will be able to direct the length and position of your cast will increase your catch rate tremendously. Another trick is to spot your fish and take note of a landmark at the edge of the river that will give you a range finder to branchmark your cast against.

BOTTOM: Malcolm Bell struggling to contain a feisty brown on a short line.

BELOW: A trophy fish heading for cover.

Lake Benmore is a great lake for shoreline stalking.

When the afternoon shadows get too long, sight fishing can become difficult; this is a good time to probe the deeper pools or fish the mouth with a streamer fly as fish move in to feed and will bite freely well into dark.

Trophy specimens tend to hang in lazy lies where food swirls past. These lies are frequently found on bends or in little side pockets and back eddies. The large fish will often be sitting in quite unusual positions in these pockets and is common to see big browns facing downstream in neutral water, which makes a downstream approach necessary if you want to avoid spooking these fish. Try and see if they will respond to dry fly or dry with a small nymph mounted on an 8 cm (3 in.) dropper. The main problem is that it can be excruciatingly difficult to get a cast to cover the fish with the drifts and flows which are short and erratic. No surprise then that these big individuals manage to grow so large and avoid the angler's hook.

Flies and Rigs

There is no need for a box filled with 50 different patterns to fish the Ahuriri River. The best flies are natural colours like Hare and Copper, Pheasant and Peacock-style nymphs both weighted and unweighted. Carrying a good supply of tungsten bead-head nymphs in sizes 12 to 16 is a must.

Much of the surface feeding occurs on sedge and mayfly but there is also a lot of random wind-blown insects like grasshoppers, bee flies and cicadas so unless a specific hatch is obvious use attractor-type dry flies. Small wet flies in sizes 10 to 14 can be deadly at dusk especially when the fish start to bulge on subsurface food rather than splashy rises to surface insects. Dark natural colours work very well, try old traditional 'wee' wet flies like Teal & Claret, Freeman's Fancy, Blue-bottle or Tup's Indispensable, they all fool trout just as well as they did a hundred years ago! For night fishing, it is hard to go past a dark-coloured size 8 Woolly Bugger.

A dark-coloured Woolly Bugger (far left) is one of the obvious flies to use when night fishing. Small Pheasant Tail nymphs (left) work on most New Zealand rivers.

Tips and Tricks

One of the best tips for fishing the Ahuriri is being able to control the depth that you fish your flies. The two keys to this are the weight of the flies and the distance they are cast above a sighted fish. You may have only a very short area of drift to cast your flies into the feeding lane of your target. Casting short with slightly heavier than normal nymphs will let you achieve this. If the water is slow and shallow, suspending your nymph or emerger beneath a dry fly will let you keep your point fly from fouling the bottom and creates a presentation that looks natural without the problem of lining the fish. In shallow water the Ahuriri fish will often take the dry-fly indicator even when there are no signs of fish feeding on the surface. Use a 3–4.5 m (10–15 ft.) tapered leader, fluorocarbon tippet and a delicate cast to minimise the chances of spooking trout that tend to become more wary as the season progresses.

Equipment and Apparel

Like many of the South Island rivers, the Ahuriri can involve walking reasonable distances in a day with multiple river crossings. The climate on any given day can be quite extreme. The morning can start at 0°C (32°F) and quickly warm to 20–30°C (68–86°F). Then a wind change from the snow-covered mountains could cool things down very rapidly.

A small good-quality day pack is great for carrying cameras and other essentials. Wading equipment such as boots, polypropylene leggings and lightweight shorts or quick-drying wading pants are ideal. Microfleece skivvies and long-sleeved shirts will offer warmth and protection from the sun. A large broad-rimmed hat protects your face

Rigging for action at the mouth of the Ahuriri.

and deflects glare, making fish spotting easier. Chapstick for your lips, SPF 20+ sunscreen and some bug repellent are all essential items. Take some nutritious food such as trail mix, muesli bars or fruit for snacking on. A good supply of fluid is also a must as dehydration can be a factor in how well you last when tramping.

For your safety, remember:
- Weather: changes can be sudden.
- Fire: Fire restrictions apply to all public conservation land. Check with the Twizel Information Centre or Department of Conservation for the current fire status.
- River crossing: Be aware of the weather in the headwaters. Do not attempt to cross swollen rivers or streams.

Flora and Fauna

The Ahuriri Conservation Park is a habitat for many bird species including the endangered black stilt, black-fronted tern and wrybill. The beech or tawhai forests are home to the main forest birds, including the threatened kea and New Zealand falcon. A wide range of native fish are present in the upper Ahuriri River, including alpine galaxias, koaro, common river galaxias and the upland bully.

Red deer, chamois and thar are all found in the park in low numbers. Chamois are more often found in scrubby bluffs and gullies above the bushline. Thar have reacted to aerial hunting by avoiding open country and now spend much of their time in bluff systems and in the scrub zone.

THINGS TO REMEMBER

DO:

- Enter the river at angler access signs. The tracks are easy to follow.
- Park off the road and away from gates.
- Work the water slowly as the fish can be very hard to spot.
- Fish different sections of the river. You will find certain areas hold more fish at different times of the year.
- Use a four-wheel-drive on the upper sections.
- Practise catch and release.

DON'T:

- Cast to a fish until you have surveyed the whole pool. There may be fish that are easier to approach.
- Fish alone for safety reasons; a rolled ankle is a lot more serious in an isolated area. Plus having a spotter will improve your ability to stalk and catch fish.
- Light fires.
- Forget to take a minute to take pictures of this magnificent area.

THINGS TO DO

The Ahuriri is truly an outdoor person's paradise and offers plenty of activities for the adventure minded traveller. From skiing to bird watching it is all here. The remoteness of the area and low population is styled to accommodate the adventure seekers. There is a good range of accommodation and places to eat in nearby areas such as Omarama or Twizel.

- Action and Adventure: There is no shortage of activities including horse trekking, three ski fields to cater to all levels of expertise, heli-ski the glaciers, 4WD biking, paragliding, gliding, skydiving, jet boating, rafting and kayaking, mountain biking, small and big game hunting, natural ice skating rink, spectacular rock and mountain climbing.
- Eco and Nature: Many rare and endangered species are found in the Ahuriri Conservation area, historic and working sheep stations are also to be found.
- Health and Relaxation: Unparalleled scenic golf courses, spas, massage, thermal pools, nature walks, scenic painting opportunities and crystal-clear star gazing.
- Arts and Gardens: museums, first-rate art and craft shopping and galleries.
- Food and Wine: Purchase fresh salmon from the farms, cafés and restaurants, wineries, wine tasting.
- Shows and Events: Omarama is well-known as great for glider flying. Many distance and time records are held here. Check with Southern Soaring as to any upcoming events.

Maps

This is a large river system. To cover the whole length in detail you will need Topographical Maps 260-G38 (Haast Pass), 260-G39 (Lake Hawea) and 260-H39 (Omarama).

Resources

Department of Conservation
Wairepo Road
Twizel
Ph: +64-3-435 0802

Twizel Information Centre
Market Place
Twizel
Ph: +64-3-435 3124

Gliding: Southern Soaring
PO Box 41
Omarama
North Otago 8950
Ph: +64-3-438 9600

The mighty Aoraki/Mt Cook, New Zealand's highest peak, as seen from Lake Tekapo.

'Often I have been exhausted on trout streams, uncomfortable, wet, cold, briar scarred, sunburned, mosquito bitten, but never, with a fly rod in my hand, have I been less than in a place that was less than beautiful.'

Charles Kuralt

WANAKA LAKES DISTRICT

11

THE ORIGIN AND MEANING OF WANAKA SEEMS TO HAVE BEEN LOST IN TIME. POSSIBLY IT IS DERIVED FROM WANANGA — SACRED KNOWLEDGE.

The travelling angler may well feel he or she has arrived in the picture-perfect postcard New Zealand as they enter the region we have called the Wanaka Lakes District. As the crow flies, all the spots mentioned here, and the literally hundreds that are not mentioned, are close together. Some, however, may be separated by ominous mountain ranges and high passes that make the driving routes rather circuitous. But this is far from an issue when you gaze at the maps and wonder how many weeks, months or years it may take to explore the rivers and lakes in what is without doubt one of the most beautiful parts of New Zealand. There is a busy lifetime's work of angling opportunities in this vicinity and we have chosen a few select waters from our many favourites in an attempt to highlight the incredible diversity of waters available to fly fishers.

For sheer volume of fish and classic South Island scenery, no trip to New Zealand would be complete without fishing the Tekapo River early in the season. You can walk along this fairy tale river, through thick patches of purple lupins and wildflowers, while hares and rabbits scamper all around. The Tekapo is rated as one of the most productive rivers in the South Island, a reputation that sees it being visited regularly by guides and anglers from around the world. A rough bumpy four-wheel-drive track that runs parallel to the river makes it possible to find new stretches of water to fish if other anglers are already fishing a section of river. As you fish or wander up the river bed, it is often difficult to keep your eyes on your fly in the panoramic vistas of snow-capped mountains and spectacular blooms of flowers all around.

At the other end of the scale, there are plenty of little gems that do not see many anglers. One of these small pieces of water is Lake Poaka, which makes a great interlude on the journey from Tekapo through to Wanaka. This tree-lined lake would be better described as a mere pond formed as a small diversion of the Twizel River. You can walk the perimeter in less than half an hour and the water is knee-deep over most of the lake. This petite still water offers excellent opportunities for ambush stalking of both rainbow and browns with the odd very respectable fish.

The region also possesses one of New Zealand's largest rivers with the highest volume in the country. The Clutha is a mighty river, big and fast, and provides a contrast to many of the other rivers in the region. At the time of writing, the Clutha has been struck with the invasive algae species commonly called 'Didymo' (*Didymosphenia geminata*), which has also been identified in several other South Island waters.

Elk Hair Caddis – when caddis are hatching, skate this fly across the surface. It is an absolute killer at dusk when the caddis hatches bring on a prolific rise.

OPPOSITE: Strolling alongside the productive Tekapo River.

Crystal-clear water, magic scenery and a fish to boot.

It can grow prolifically on riverbeds and its further spread is highly undesirable. So ensure you clean, decontaminate and dry your equipment when fishing these waters!

Lake Wanaka and Lake Hawea are two of the district's large showcase still waters and have plenty of fishing options from shore and boat. Topographical maps of the region detail the great number of rivers that enter the lakes and many of these are very productive, especially the Hunter River, Timaru Creek and Matukituki River.

At the top end of Lake Wanaka – as you head towards Haast Pass and the West Coast – is the Makarora River. Like so many South Island rivers the Makarora is braided from where it enters Lake Wanaka right up to where it enters the Haast Pass. Towering over the river is the snowcapped peaks of Mt Alba and Mt Pollux, which make up part of Mt Aspiring National Park. The lower

reaches hold stocks of rainbow and brown trout that can be sight fished in the waters that can at times be some of the clearest you will ever see. Fishing access to the river is beside the road and through farmland right up through the Haast Pass. This stretch of water has a good one or two days' fishing and is another area that you can find yourself fishing by yourself on most week days.

Converging with the Makarora is the Wilkin River, which has a hiking trail that is popular with trampers, hunters and anglers looking to get off the beaten track. Jet boats also can take explorers up and drop them off for a couple of days to enjoy the Wilkin and to experience its superb fishing.

The Wanaka Lake District covers a large area and provides a wide range of fly-fishing options with both rivers and lakes in abundance. The scenic qualities of this region are truly outstanding and provide a backdrop to an ideal location if you wish to fish and take part in many of the unique and adventurous activities in the South Island.

Getting there

For the international angler, the nearest airport to this region is in Queenstown. To make getting to each spot easy we have identified the closest town, city or landmark to help with your travels. Be aware that these areas are very spread out when travelling by road.

Tekapo River

Twizel is the closest township to the Tekapo River. Although there are some access roads that are direct they would not be recommended for the average traveller. The favoured route is to turn off State Highway 8 between Lake Tekapo and Fairlie at a Junction named 'Dog Kennel Corner'. This route takes you along a metal (gravel road) alongside the Grays River to the Haldon Camp. From here you can access the river by driving or walking. The road is suitable for 4x4 vehicles only. Trails along this road lead to different parts of the Tekapo river.

Lake Poaka

Travelling just south on State Highway 8, you reach the Pukakai/Ohau Canal and just off to the right before the bridge over the canal is a gravel side road. This will take you to Lake Poaka.

Clutha River

The easiest access for the mighty Clutha is the road between Wanaka and Lake Hawea at Albert Town where access is easy via the campground or tracks alongside the river on the opposite bank. Alternatively you can head out east on either State Highway 6 or 8a and pick up the river at several points along either route.

Lake Wanaka and Lake Hawea

If you head west on State Highway 6, the road runs between Lake Hawea and Lake Wanaka. At

Lake Hawea junction you can decide to head off towards Gladstone to fish the rivers and western shoreline of Lake Hawea or continue along State Highway 6 to reach the eastern end of Lake Wanaka and the Makarora River.

Access

One of the features of this region is the ease of access to good sites. While a four-wheel-drive vehicle is really warranted for exploring some of the river tracks, you can get to most spots in a sedan or campervan. A detailed map showing tracks and access points is invaluable.

Wildflowers in full bloom.

BELOW: Lake Poaka

ABOVE: Wildflowers, especially lupins, put on a spectacular display through the MacKenzie country.

ABOVE RIGHT: Fish tend to lie in the skinny water.

Angling

Because the Wanaka Lakes District covers many different types of water, the key is to be able to adapt quickly to suit the conditions. The chief angling skills to concentrate on are stalking the fish, casting accuracy and presentation. Get these skills right and you will be rewarded with fish that will take your offerings freely. Get it wrong and you will be frustrated by refusals and fish fleeing for the nearest cover.

Tekapo River

Fishing the Tekapo River is a sheer delight. The size and depth of this semi-braided system make wading and crossing very easy. The fish tend to lie very tight to the banks and right at the heads of pools in what would have to be called very skinny water. I remember catching one brown in a little offshoot of the river that had been crossed by my fishing companions. It was no more than a rivulet that could be stepped across. I threw a Royal Wulff just to the edge of the main current and it was grabbed instantly by a fish in the 2.5 kg (5 lb.) class. That's the thing with the Tekapo River – you really have to keep alert and look for fish.

The Tekapo has a large concentration of mayfly and caddis. Imitations that work well are

CDC Mayfly, Royal Wulff and Adams, while slim nymphs with a little weight like Pheasant Tail and latex Caddis work well for subsurface fishing. Another good tip is to trail an emerger patter on a dropper with a dry fly as fish may appear to be rising when they are actually taking just below the surface and in the film.

Lake Poaka

Both rainbow and brown trout can be spotted cruising and feeding in the clear water. It is quite unnerving to have a fly lying motionless as a fish casually swims towards it from some distance away. It is worth spending half a day chasing fish around this lake. The visual aspect of a fish caught here will stick with you for a lifetime. The best technique is to spot a fish and watch the beat or route that it is working. When the fish is swimming away or far enough away that is won't be frightened, cast out a small dry fly and dropper rig. A small Humpy with a size 14 Hare and Copper is a good choice. Let this settle and wait for the fish to return on its beat. Sometimes the slightest of moves will see the fish swimming off to the other side of the lake. If everything comes together, the fish will swim up behind your fly and you will see its mouth open to take your fly. Don't forget to strike!

Clutha River

Fishing the Clutha during a sedge (caddis) hatch is quite an experience. You may be casting large Caddis dry flies into the swirling current in the darkness as you hear pops and splashes all around from fish feeding freely. Suddenly, you will be connected to a hard-fighting fish in fast water.

For a unique experience take a look at the river around Albert Town, where there are various places to access the river. The campground is a good area to prospect. Don't be surprised if you come across schools of fish holding in the current and freely rising around the pines. Walking upstream from the camp, or driving around to the other bank, will show you the great variety of fishable water.

Lakes Wanaka and Hawea

Fishing Lakes Wanaka and Hawea is great fun. Shoreline stalking can be very rewarding, and one of the most popular spots is Paddock Bay. Fishing wet flies around any of the river mouths, especially at night, can also be spectacular.

These lakes hold a good population of landlocked Chinook salmon, which adds variety to catches. The Chinook grow to a couple of kilos and are spirited fighters. The best way to target them is to fish with lure-type wet flies on sinking lines when they are feeding on smelt around the river mouths.

Makarora River

Stalking the sandy flats where the river enters the lake can make for a lot of fun. Casting small wet flies and nymph to the cruising fish as they forage will get the pulse racing. The wind plays a big factor in this type of fishing as the winds around this region can be quite fickle.

The Clutha River is big water that holds plenty of trout for the keen angler.

Adam with a bonus
from Lake Hawea:
a land-locked
Chinook salmon.

Season

The regulations vary across the different waters in the region. The easiest way to check which waters are open is to check the Fish and Game website (www.fishandgame.org.nz) or visit one of the local tackle stores.

Techniques and Tactics

The different waters all offer their own little quirks to fish, but all can be approached in much the same way. A mixture of nymph and dry-fly fishing will produce results. The key tactic is to find out what insect life is most prevalent at the time. You may get a consistent hatch of mayfly during the day and have to look for feeding lanes, whereas at night if the sedge get going you may as well not even start fishing until dusk.

Flies and Rigs

Due to the abundance of insect life in this region, it would pay to have a well-stocked fly box. A couple of necessities are a Deer Hair Caddis dry in sizes 10 to 12 and a good size range of Adams Irresistible. A very successful rig when the sedge are coming off is to trail a small soft-hackle wet fly behind a Deer Hair Caddis dry on a leader that is greased and allow them to slowly swing downstream at the end of a drift. Control the speed of the swing by letting out a bit of loose line as they arc across the current.

Tips and Tricks

Fishing the Wanaka Lakes District has many varieties of fishing opportunities and one of the most important tips for success is to pay careful attention to the weather patterns. The wind can have a very strong influence on where you should decide to fish. To make matters even more interesting, this region has unpredictable weather with micro-environments caused by the vast ranges and varying temperatures. Lake Wanaka can have a stiff breeze forming white caps up the lake, while Lake Hawea can be mirror calm. As a rule of thumb, fishing into a stiff breeze can be very difficult on the lakes and makes spotting cruising fish nearly impossible. Find a bluff or a piece of sheltered water nearby and you will be able to cast and spot fish with ease; the swirling wind causes currents in the lakes that are natural feeding spots for trout. The rivers feature some of the clearest water you will ever see. This clarity also affords trout plenty of time to inspect offerings from anglers. Try and use the longest leaders possible and keep breaking strains as light as practicable. Before each cast, inspect flies to ensure they are sitting properly with no debris on the hook. Always maintain a very low profile and avoid casting shadows onto the water. If a fish refuses a fly that is in its feeding lane, let the fish rest for a minute, then change flies to a smaller pattern and try again.

When lake fishing, the depth of the drop-off and how close it comes to shore is very important as this is the prime feeding zone in most lakes. If the lake drops away quickly there will be very

Dry and dropper rigs are deadly. Make sure your flies are sitting properly with the point down, unlike the one pictured here.

little area for fish to hunt, making it less attractive to them. Alternatively, if there is a good area of shallows before the lake gets deeper this is highly attractive to fish. Another type of site that is very productive when lake fishing is any region where water flows into the lake. This could be in the form of a stream or even a little stormwater drain. Trout will always congregate near moving water.

Fishing during change of light is certainly very productive when lakes fishing as the fish tend to be less wary and move in to feed with the added cover of darkness. At this time changing from nymphs to a dark-coloured wet fly slowly retrieved over the drop-off is the way to go.

Capturing the moment.

A typical Otago landscape.

Lake Wanaka is surrounded by native shrub land, featuring kanuka and manuka, (species of ti tree). Mount Aspiring National Park is a mountainous terrain with pastoral farmland, beech forests, alpine tussock grasslands and snowfields. Many varieties of beech tree including Southern, Red, Mountain and Silver Beech are all represented within the park.

Many native New Zealand and introduced birds and animals grace this exquisite terrain. Ten of the 51 species of native birds that inhabit the areas around Lake Wanaka are classified as rare. Avid bird watchers would keep a look out for the New Zealand falcon (karearea), blue duck (whio), New Zealand pigeon (kereru), kaka, yellow crowned parakeet (kakariki) and kea.

Other species of note include New Zealand's only native mammal, the long tailed bat, numerous native fish and abundant invertebrates including 400 species of butterflies and many lizards.

Flora and Fauna

Lake Wanaka is the gateway to Mt Aspiring National Park. The park, Lake Wanaka and the surrounding areas are pristine environments encompassing a diverse range of habitats and wilderness areas.

THINGS TO REMEMBER

DO:

- Allow plenty of time to explore this marvellous region.
- Try a different spot each day to experience the different experiences they offer. You can always revisit your favourites.
- Employ a guide for a couple of days. Guides provide a rapid learning experience of access spots and techniques that can save a lot of wasted time and effort.
- Keep a daily journal of your fishing. This is a great way to record vital information such as successful flies, maps on how to access areas, people's names and contacts who you meet along the way.

DON'T:

- Fish until you have checked the local regulations.
- Leave waders and gear unwashed as you move to different waters.
- Forget to book accommodation. This is an extremely popular area for all sorts of activities.
- Enter areas without obtaining permission. Most people are very obliging and often share valuable fishing information.

THINGS TO DO

The Wanaka Lakes District is one of the best in New Zealand for all kinds of activities. That is why we recommend that plenty of time be allocated to this region. Not only does it have fantastic fishing, the stunning vistas of the lakes and snow capped peaks are unparalleled and the activities and attractions are plentiful.

The Wanaka and Mackenzie region always has plenty of opportunity to participate in events and activities – from jet boating to bungy-jumping to enjoying a quiet one at the historic Cardrona Hotel.

- Shows and Events: Wanaka Rodeo – the thrills and spills of rodeo action; Upper Clutha Agricultural and Pastoral Show – the second largest agricultural show in the South island; Warbirds Over Wanaka – historic aircraft, Royal New Zealand Air Force jets, aerobatic formations, helicopters and fun for all the family at Wanaka airport; Race to the Sky – an international hill climb at Waiorau Snow Farm; The World HeliChallenge – an annual gathering of the world's leading snowboarders and skiers takes the term 'free-riding' to the edge; Pulsate Wanaka Big Air – join the fun and action in downtown Wanaka as the world's premier aerialists of skiing and boarding take flight.

Maps

This is a vast territory and most anglers will only require a detailed road map. However, anyone venturing into the back country should acquire the correct Topographical Map for the region (see: www.linz.govt.nz/rcs/linz/ pub/web/root/core/Topography/TopographicMaps/ 260mapindex)

Resources

Lake Wanaka Visitor Information Centre
The Log Cabin, Lakefront,
100 Ardmore Street, Wanaka
Ph: +64-3-443 1233
Fax: +64-3-443 1290
Email: info@lakewanaka.co.nz
Web: www.lakewanaka.co.nz

Department of Conservation
Lake Wanaka Area Office
Lake Wanaka
Ph: +64-3-443 7660
Fax: +64-3-443 8777

Field Centre Makarora
Ph: +64-3-443 8365
Fax: +64-3-443 8374

Wilkin River Jets
Makarora
Ph: +64-3-443 8351
Email: info@wilkinriverjets.co.nz
www.fishandgame.org.nz

- Action and Adventure: Ski Treble Cone, ice skating, heli-skiing glaciers.
- 4WD driving and biking, paragliding, gliding,skydiving, jet boating, rafting and kayaking, mountain biking, small and big game hunting, climbing of all disciplines including bouldering, rock climbing and alpine climbing.
- Eco and Nature: Visit the Gates of Haast, lake cruises, eco and nature adventures.
- Health and Relaxation: Golf course, Wanaka has a top range of resorts and health spas catering for everything from relaxation, recreation or just improving your general well-being.
- Arts and Gardens: Museums, first-rate art and craft shopping and galleries
- Food and Wine: A wide range of dining experiences to suit every palate and budget; vineyards, restaurants, and cafés.

The beautiful Mataura River.

'If you wish happiness for an hour, get intoxicated. If you wish happiness for three days, get married. If you wish happiness for eight days, kill a pig and eat it. If you wish happiness forever, then learn to fish...'

Ancient Chinese proverb, author unknown

MATAURA RIVER

12

Mataura — reddish, eddying water. The swamp water which drains into the river is impregnated with iron oxide.

Situated in the lower half of the South Island, the Mataura makes a great starting point for anglers fishing the South Island. With a large population of good-sized trout and the sheer variety of insect life that they feed on, it is the ideal river on which to gain an initial understanding, and to get you ready to take up the challenges of what the rest of the South Island waters have to offer. When fishing in the Mataura, you will hone your spotting, casting and stalking skills, which are vitally important when fishing in the South Island. You will use a variety of techniques that will serve you well for most other rivers. Most importantly, the reputation of the Mataura for producing excellent fishing is well earned and not to be missed by keen visiting anglers.

Stalking the slightly tannin-coloured Mataura is a pleasure. It is one of those rivers that looks as if it had been designed by an angler; with deep pools and rapids and fish-holding structures around every bend—the sort of place where you can't wait to see what the next pool has to offer. Careful spotting and accurate casting will see an angler catching fish from 1 to 2.5 kg (2.2 to 5 lb.) fairly consistently. The Mataura does hold large fish and trophy specimens are caught each year, although if you were trying to target a large specimen, the Mataura would not be at the top of the list.

The mayfly hatch on the Mataura is world famous and casting to rising fish can be enjoyed all day in the right conditions at the right time of year. Judicious choice of fly pattern, leader weight and length will play a big part on how well the offering is accepted. When fishing to subsurface feeders, your skill-set has to be expanded as spotting fish in coloured water that seems to be

custom-made for camouflaging the brown trout, will see heavy-footed anglers frightening fish. I have seen a cast into no more than a few inches of water turn into a solid strike, and the first time the fish was sighted was when the white of its belly flashed.

Blue Dun – when trout rising to mayfly ignore all other offerings, try this fly. Stick to small sizes in the 12 to 16 range.

LEFT: You need to focus and train your eye to spot these well-camouflaged fish!

OPPOSITE: The Mataura has a reputation for fine fishing.

ABOVE AND RIGHT:
There is a huge variety of water to suit the taste of every fly angler.

The Mataura winds for some 190 km (118 miles) in length, and the major part of the river is fishable right down to the sea. The headwaters are located in mountains to the south of Lake Wakatipu. From there it flows south-east towards Gore, where it turns southward. It then passes through the town of Mataura, and enters the Pacific Ocean at Toetoes Bay on the southern coast of the South Island.

Getting There

Because of the length of the river, there are many choices on how you get to the fishing waters of the Mataura. Here are a few suggestions that should be considered when planning your trip. From Christchurch International Airport you can transfer to a domestic flight with the most

An aerial view of very 'fishy' water from the comfort of Nokomai Station's helicopter.

convenient destination airport being Invercargill, 1 hour and 15 minutes by air from Christchurch. The journey to Gore takes about one hour from Invercargill by car.

The most convenient way to travel by air to target the upper Mataura River, is to catch a domestic flight to Queenstown and drive south from Lake Wakatipu on State Highway 6. The closest international airport is in Dunedin (with limited international arrivals), and it is approximately 150 km (93 miles) by road to Gore. Driving is a pleasant alternative if time allows. The roads are good and well signposted, and driving will give you a chance to see the countryside. Be warned: you may be forced to make lots of pit stops to check out the rivers that abound in this region, and to photograph the magnificent scenery.

Access

Access throughout the length of the Mataura River is generally good. Some places are marked by Fish and Game signs while other spots may not be so clearly defined. If in doubt, it pays to ask the locals. There are several good sources for specific access information including the Fish and Game website and John Kent's excellent travel guides, which we highly recommend to anglers (see bibliography).

A reasonable brown under the gaze of the hunter.

ABOVE: We like to tie our Hare and Coppers fairly messily, with plenty of scraggly tufts of hare dubbing protruding.

RIGHT: The proof of the pudding is in the catching!

Season

- Mataura River and tributaries upstream of Humes Road Bridge, Garston: a trophy trout zone – all fish larger than 40 cm (16 in.) must be returned. Season runs from 1 October to 30 April. Limit one fish under 40 cm.
- Garston Bridge to Gore Bridge: 1 October to 30 April. Limit four fish.
- Gore Bridge to the Gorge Road Bridge: 1 October to 31 May. Limit four fish.
- Gorge Road Bridge to sea: Year-round fishing. Limit four fish.

Use dull, natural, earth-coloured flies in smaller sizes.

Techniques and Tactics

Tactically, one of the most important factors to consider when fishing the Mataura is what the fish are feeding on and at what stage of the life cycle the insect is at. Careful observation, capturing insects, or examining the stomach contents of fish will give you an idea of their diet. Be aware that throughout the day conditions will change and affect how fish are feeding. For example, just after a hatch you may get an abundance of spent spinners in quiet back waters and this is where you will find the larger fish making the most of easy foraging. Adding a very small natural-coloured indicator can help sight flies in deep pools, but in good conditions you will be casting to sighted fish and will be looking for telltale signs such as a fish moving back to take flies or the flash of white when the mouth opens to take the fly.

Flies and Rigs

Accurate size and style imitations will result in the best fishing. When it comes to flies, mayfly dries in the earthy tones in sizes 12 to 16 are the killers. It is hard to go past a Dad's Favourite either in the traditional style or the parachute variant. When

the fish are feeding on the subsurface, try sizes 12 to 16 Pheasant and Peacock nymphs or very sparsely tied Hare and Coppers that have a touch of weight. During the warmer months cicadas, grasshoppers and willow grubs will also be on the menu and a few good imitations along those lines are worth inclusion in the fly box.

When prospecting the Mataura, a dry and dropper rig will cover most pools. In the shallower stretches tie the dry on as the tail fly and let the nymph suspend below a branch dropper about 20 to 30 cm (8 to 12 in.) long. In the deeper stretches, or if there is no visible surface activity, fish a pair of nymphs, including a small tungsten bead-head nymph above an unweighted Hare and Copper. Keeping leaders and tippets light will attract more strikes and provide good sport on the Mataura River. If you feel comfortable with it, using a 2 kg (4.4 lb.) tippet is well worth the effort.

Tips and Tricks

Take time to look for fish. You will find them holding in some very interesting places. Anywhere there is a subtle depression in the riverbed is fish-holding water. The biggest fish always tend to hold in the best lies and often in difficult areas to cast. Don't be afraid to throw a long cast across fast water into slow water where a fish is holding. If the fish is feeding properly you only need a short drift to invoke a strike. Try not to go into the water, and avoid sudden movements. When entering a pool, put in a few short casts in the unlikely-looking spots first to get your range and check the drift, and because you will quite

THIS PAGE: A careful approach, appropriate fly selection and a delicate cast accounted for this chubby specimen.

RIGHT: Willows provide the ideal ambush territory for the Mataura river angler.

often see fish that you did not spot at first.

There are large stands of willows lining the banks along much of the river and this vegetation provides shade, food and ideal ambush territory for the trout. These are great zones to drift dries or nymphs – the closer the better.

Equipment and Apparel

The Mataura is pretty easy going, being fairly flat with easy walking. Anglers can wet wade or use lightweight breathable waders. This is one place where it is very useful to wear good camouflage clothing and carry amber-coloured Polaroid glasses.

RIGHT: Polaroid glasses help to spot a good catch.

Flora and Fauna

This area would have to offer the most diverse flora and fauna compared to any other region in New Zealand. With landscapes ranging from lush pastures and rolling meadows to inland fiords and alpine ranges. There is a wealth of rare interesting plants and creatures, the likes of which should satisfy any nature lover. Of particular interest is the number of rare and endangered bird species including the only known population of rock wren (piwauwau) outside the Southern Alps. A widespread population of falcon (karearea), kea, native pigeon (kereru) and yellow-crowned parakeet (kakariki).

Unique invertebrate fauna such as the giant land snail, the giant speargrass weevil and a stronghold for the 'inch and half ground beetle'.

A good variety of lizard species, both geckos and skinks co-exist with native fish and domestic livestock and feral animals such as deer and rabbits.

THINGS TO REMEMBER

DO:

- Try to match the hatch.
- Ask landowners permission before proceeding.
- Check the weather forecast.
- Take insect repellent, sunscreen and food. Wear dull clothing as the fish are easily spooked especially as the season progresses.
- Take a good selection of fly sizes, weights and patterns (size 10–16).

DON'T:

- Attempt river crossings in high water flows or if you are inexperienced.
- Leave any rubbish, food scraps or discarded monofilament.
- Expect to fish next to your car in the upper reaches.
- Leave gates open or interfere with livestock. This will be the quickest way to have access denied for all future anglers.

THINGS TO DO

Over its 190 km (118 mile) course to the sea, the Mataura flows through a wide variety of landscapes ranging from large stations (big farms in the South Island are called stations), through tracts of native bush before it finally flows into the sea. Some of the stations provide accommodation and a wide range of activities should you need a break from catching fish. If you get a chance, visit one of the local pubs, enjoy a beer, and listen to the yarns told by some of the characters that live in this part of the world.

- Action and Adventure: Mountain biking, hunting, horse trekking, 4WD adventures, snow-mobiling, jet boating.
- Eco and Nature: Farm stays, scenic helicopter trips, train excursions (Kingston Flyer), nature trails and bush walks within Fiordland National Park, historic homesteads.
- Health and Relaxation: Camping, picnics, museums.
- Arts and Gardens: Local art and craft shops.
- Food and Wine: Restaurants serving local delicacies like whitebait fritters and paua (a form of abalone), pubs and cafés.

Nokomai Station, one of the country's largest, offers splendid accommodation, meals and guided fishing, with over 20 km (12 miles) of the Mataura River flowing through the property.

Maps

You can easily get by with a good road map, but for those interested in more detail the best Topographical Map covering the upper and middle sections is 260-E44 (Lumsden).

Resources
Gore Information Centre
Norfolk Street
Gore
Ph: +64-3-208 9908
Fax: +64-3-208 9908
Email: goreinfo@esi.co.nz
Web: www.mataura.com

Department of Conservation
Southland Conservancy Office
State Insurance Building
7th Floor, Don Street
Invercargill
Tel: +64-3-214 4589
Fax: +64-3-214 4486

Nokomai Helicopters
Provide access to many remote river systems in Southland.
James Hore
Ph: +64-3-248 8895 or +64-3-248 8825
Email: nokomai.helicopters@xtra.co.nz
Web: www.nokomai.co.nz

www.fishandgame.org.nz
(Key words Southland and Mataura)

References

Like so many travelling anglers, we have found John Kent's trout fishing guides to the North Island and South Island to be invaluable travel bibles and a source of both inspiration and thoroughly researched reference material. Other useful sources include:

New Zealand Fish and Game information booklets and website (www.fishandgame.org.nz).
Department of Conservation publications and website (www.doc.govt.nz).
New Zealand Professional Fishing Guides Association (www.nzpfga.com).

Bibliography

- Harris, Brian *The Art of Flyfishing*. Ward Lock Ltd, London, 1980.
- Kent, John *North Island Trout Fishing Guide*. Reed Books, Auckland, 1995.
- Kent, John *South Island Trout Fishing Guide*. Reed Books, Auckland, 2004.
- New Zealand Mountain Safety Council Inc. *Mountain Safety Manual 31,* 2000.
- Prosek, James *Trout of the World*. Stewart, Tabori and Chang, New York, 2003.
- Reed, A.W. *The Reed Dictionary of Maori Place Names*. Reed Books, Auckland, 2005.
- Williams, A. Courtney *A Dictionary of Trout Flies and of Flies for Sea-Trout and Grayling*. Adam and Charles Black, London, 1949.

Picturesque pocket water in the middle reaches of the Ohinemuri.